BREAKTHROUGH
ANOINTING

Divine Strategies for
a Life of Spiritual Power

LaNora
Van Arsdall

Chosen Books

A Division of Baker Book House Co
Grand Rapids, Michigan 49516

Published by Chosen Books
a division of Baker Book House Company
P.O. Box 6287, Grand Rapids, MI 49516-6287
www.bakerbooks.com

Printed in the United States of America

Library of Congress Cataloging-in-Publication Data
Van Arsdall, LaNora, 1953–
    Breakthrough anointing : divine strategies for a life of spiritual
power / LaNora Van Arsdall.
        p.   cm.
    ISBN 0-8007-9332-3 (pbk.)
    1. Christian women—Religious life. 2. Spiritual life—Christianity.
I. Title.
BV4527.V355 2003
243—dc21   2003003597

To Dr. Fuchsia Pickett, my mother in the faith. You imparted the deep desire to know Him more and to "dig for silver"—the hidden mysteries of the Word. I am eternally grateful.

To Dr. Judson Cornwall, my father in the faith. You patiently walked me through some of the hardest changes of my life by showing me the Father's heart. Forever I will treasure the wisdom of your counsel and the secrets I learned by listening to you pray.

Contents

FOREWORD

The words of *Breakthrough Anointing* will simply leap off the page to those who are hungry for revival. LaNora Van Arsdall has done the Body of Christ a great service. She has distilled the cry of our hearts to see both personal and corporate revival.

Few people have the ability to put this heart cry onto the printed page, but LaNora has done just that. Her words simply melt deep into one's soul.

My preacher daddy used to make a statement that has stayed with me. He would say that sometimes we need to find the thing that will scratch what itches. All of us have that deep need to read and understand how to move toward the Father in a way that will release the abundant life that has been promised to us.

It is wonderful to know that we do not just have to struggle and survive in this world. The Christian life is much more than simply living day after day and holding on. Our life should be full of God-filled, supernatural adventure. Some are not experiencing this abundant life because they do not know how to experience the breakthroughs necessary to reach that point.

My friend, open the pages of this book and get ready for God to change your heart and life. You will not finish its contents the same person.

Cindy Jacobs, co-founder
Generals of Intercession
Colorado Springs, Colorado

ACKNOWLEDGMENTS

M y heartfelt gratitude to:
Barbara Boyd for the countless hours of intercession and untiring labor of love on this book. Your friendship is priceless and eternal. Only God knows the price
you have paid. May it count for glory!

Pastors Bob and Susan Beckett for believing in me, pressing me to the goal and covering me with grace. You and
the Dwelling Place Family Church are a haven to me.

Rev. Faye Darnell for encouraging me to answer the call
of God on my life and for setting such a beautiful example
for me to follow.

Dr. Dianne McIntosh who weeps with me, rejoices with
me, prays for me, counsels me, and always points me to
Jesus. You taught me the secret of heart change—the kind
that lasts. Your friendship is a precious treasure.

Carol Noe for your encouragement and hard work in the
beginning days of editing.

Melanie Shaner, my beloved daughter and friend. You
are an exquisite example of one who embraces change with
courage. You inspire me.

Kari and Tim Thompson, my precious daughter and son-in-law, my pastors, and my friends. When others told me to quit, you believed in God's purposes.

Dr. Iverna Tompkins who challenged me to live a life of radical obedience. I thank God and you for the time I spent serving the Lord in your ministry. I received your instruction as oil upon my head.

Fountaingate Staff and Team for the prayers and personal sacrifices to make this book possible. Together we will continue to open city gates to the King of Glory!

Fountain Of Life Fellowship, my church family, for your powerful example of the breakthrough anointing. As you exalt Him to the highest place of honor, lives are transformed and the desert blooms. You are a place of refreshing and revival to me.

Umpa for your Godly life and example. To me, you looked like Jesus. I miss you.

Dan Van Arsdall, my husband, for pointing me to the Holy Spirit and for teaching me many things. I am changed forever.

The Tuesday Night Prayer Group for your intercession and perseverance in times of incredible warfare. You are forever in my heart.

Jane Campbell and Ann Weinheimer for the countless hours of editing and for your wisdom and Christlike patience with me.

INTRODUCTION

I anticipated the dawning of the morning and cried [in childlike prayer]; I hoped in Your word.

PSALM 119:147 (AMP)

The day of God's power and the coming forth of a new generation is upon us. Even as a woman nearing the birth of her child feels that she cannot go on one more day in her pregnant condition, so it is with us. A day is about to be born. We feel its pressure in our spiritual wombs. From the moment the Divine Seed of Light, Jesus Christ, was planted within us, we have grown full of His purposes for our lives. Those individuals who have yielded to the process of His life within them will join in the corporate purpose of bringing to birth a new day. If we look upon the horizon with spiritual eyes, we can see it dawning. As the earth is growing darker with the effects of sin, there is a bright rising of His glory in the Church (see Isaiah 60:1–2). The day of His power is a day of His glory revealed to the nations.

This is a book written for a hungry people to confirm the stirrings of anticipation and expectation that are even now within them. It is written for a people who are "pregnant" with their personal destinies and with the "last days" revival. As you read, it is my prayer that the Morning Star will rise in your heart. May His brightness break through upon you like the noonday sun!

ONE

"WHO TOUCHED ME?"

For she was saying to herself, "If I only touch His garment, I will get well."

MATTHEW 9:21

L ife was going great for me—or so anyone watching would have thought. It was 1981 and my world seemed picture-perfect. My husband, Dan, had just been hired as one of the staff pastors of a "megachurch" of five thousand members. We had two beautiful daughters, a new home and money in the bank. Everyone, including my family, thought I was happy and fulfilled. What more could a woman want?

However . . . things were not as they seemed. I was empty inside. I felt growing discontentment and frustration that I did not comprehend. I felt guilty that I was not satisfied; should I not "count my blessings," as my mother used to say? This inner conflict drove me to my knees and launched me on a quest—a search for God's purposes for my life. Being a wife and mother was a tremendous source of joy, but I knew that deep inside of me was a destiny that was yet to be revealed. My identity was very much encompassed by my roles. I tried to ignore my feelings of dissatisfaction, but they would not go away.

One evening, just before a Bible study at our church, I found myself at a crossroads. God seized an ordinary family occurrence and used it to stir me to pursue my personal breakthrough. One of Dan's pastoral responsibilities was to lead the Friday night weekly study for about one hundred single people. That night we were running late. I was rushing our daughters out of the house when four-year-old Melanie dropped her big carton of 32 crayons all over the floor. She sat down and started to pick them up, one by one, and put them back into the carton. When Dan saw the mess and the delay it was causing, he raised his voice and said firmly, "Hurry up! We've got to go! We're going to be late!" Melanie hurriedly grabbed the remaining crayons with her little hands, put the box under her arm and ran to the car.

I cannot explain exactly what happened to me at that moment, but something snapped. For a split second, I felt as though I was the little girl who was in trouble. I began to cry uncontrollably. Dan was dumbfounded; my reaction to his comments was beyond reason. As we drove to the church, he tried to comfort me but I could not stop crying. Dan took the girls and went on to the meeting. I slipped into the church office to try to pull myself together. As I sat in the quiet room contemplating what had just happened, I realized in a flash that something had to change. Specifically, someone had to change . . . and that someone was me.

On the church staff was a minister whom I had grown to love and to appreciate for her wisdom. Somehow I believed that she would help me understand my bizarre behavior and with it my general unhappiness. I picked up the office phone to call Faye Darnell. My quest had begun.

Faye listened patiently as I poured out my heart. I told her of my nagging fears and the sense of frustration with my life. I shared the events of the evening with her and wondered if she thought I needed professional help.

"What was that all about?" I asked. "Why did I become the little girl who was in trouble?" My heart pounded as I waited for her response. Faye suggested gently that I probably had some unresolved childhood issues that needed healing. She said that the Lord wanted to use situations such as the one that I had just experienced to reveal those issues. She then prayed a simple prayer and asked the Lord to continue the process even in my sleep.

A DREAM THAT CHANGED MY LIFE

That same night, I had a powerful dream that awakened painful memories and unlocked the door to my confusion. Later, as I studied the Scriptures to which this dream related, I discovered how barriers keep us from fulfilling our personal destinies in God. The keys I found helped me to be released from difficulties of my past and to *break through* to the future that God had ordained for me.[1] In my dream—and what God taught me through it— I received wonderful revelation about how to live victoriously in Christ. It changed my life.

I dreamed that I was present as an observer when the woman with the issue of blood reached out to touch Jesus (see Mark 5:25–34; Luke 8:41–48). It happened when Jesus was walking with His disciples in the midst of a large crowd to the house of Jairus to pray for his daughter who was dying.

In my dream I saw this woman in her pain and anguish straining to see Jesus, pushing through the crowd with determination that revealed her desperation. She knew there was no hope of help from doctors or any other source. Then, rather than being an onlooker with others in the crowd, I became the woman with the issue of blood. It was I who came up behind Him and reached out to touch His cloak, believing that I would be healed if I succeeded in doing so.

Suddenly Jesus stopped and asked His disciples who had touched Him. His disciples responded, as we might have, that with all these people pressing around Him, who could tell? They did not realize what Jesus meant—that there was more than one way to touch Him. Jesus knew that someone had touched Him *with faith*. He knew it because He felt healing virtue go out of Him.

I remember wishing anxiously that the camera of my dream would pan around so that I could see the face of Jesus. It did not. I never saw His face, but I had felt the terrible desperation in that woman's heart as she dared to push her way through the throngs of people and reach out to Him. I had experienced her thrill as His healing power shot through her body. I had felt her astonishment, her awe and her gratitude at being set free from her issue of blood.

As I awoke from this dream, the Holy Spirit said to me: *LaNora, become like this woman. Don't let the crowds of people keep you from getting to Jesus with the issues of your life. Don't look to men for answers or fear their reproach. Determine to touch Jesus.*

When I went to the Bible to review the touching story of this daring woman, I began to understand better the obstacles she had to overcome to experience her breakthrough into personal healing. This woman had suffered from hemorrhaging for twelve years, had endured much at the hands of doctors and had spent all her money for treatment, only to find her condition growing worse (see Mark 5:25–26).

Her plight was made even more humiliating because of the demands of Jewish law. According to the Law of Moses, if a woman suffered from an issue of blood she was considered unclean; everything and everyone she touched was defiled by her (see Leviticus 15:25–27). The social isolation that resulted from having a condition like this for years must have caused her as much grief as the physical weakness and discomfort.

In her determination to receive help from Jesus, help that no one else could promise her, this Jewish woman was driven to violate the social law of her culture. She would not be deterred in her attempt to touch Jesus, this rabbi whose reputation for healing she knew. If she could only touch His garment! Perhaps she hoped that touching just the fringe would not defile Him. If there was the slightest chance she could be healed by His divine power, she had to try. Her plan required her to press through a crowd of people. Surely this would mean defiling them also . . . but she pressed on.

In an instant her anguish ceased! As soon as she abandoned all protocol and reached out to touch Jesus' garment, she felt the healing power of God flow through her body. But then new fears arose: She had not escaped notice. When Jesus said, "Who touched Me?" she knew that she would have to confess her sin and her unclean condition to this holy Man in front of this crowd of people. What would His reaction be? And the people's reaction? Would they cast her out? Would He? Trembling, she came and fell down before Jesus and told Him the whole truth.

As I read Jesus' words to her, I remembered from my dream the unspeakable thrill of her heart at the Master's tender commendation: "Daughter, your faith has made you well; go in peace and be healed of your affliction" (Mark 5:34). What most considered to be a violation of the religious law of the day had resulted in a breakthrough for a hopeless condition. Her attempt to reach Jesus was hailed by the Master as an act of faith.

The dream lingered with me for a while. As I considered the way this woman broke through the barriers of the crowd, abandoned socially acceptable behavior and defied her sense of personal dignity to get to Jesus, I began to ask myself some hard questions. What were the things in my life that hindered me from getting to Jesus? What was keeping me from getting to God with my "issues"? How could I get the answers I needed for my own painful, destructive life patterns? What was keeping me from breaking through to my personal destiny in God?

I thought about the words of the Holy Spirit to me, that I was to become like this woman. What did that mean for me personally? How could I experience that sheer abandonment of social and personal convention in order to get to Jesus for my personal breakthrough? As I have waited before God and searched the Scriptures, I have found answers to these questions.

Throughout this book I will be sharing with you those answers, those keys that have unlocked the purposes of my life. I hope that they will touch your life as well.

PASSION FOR CHANGE

My dream had an enormous impact on me when I realized that I was like the woman in this story in many ways.

In my own feeling of desperation I, too, had run out of options.

Sometimes I delayed coming to Jesus because I put confidence in human counsel, much as this woman looked to the doctors of her day. Inevitably, people disappointed me because they could not give me the remedy I sought. When I pursued various self-help methods, I discovered that they did not bring lasting deliverance either.

It is true that God had spoken to me many times through the counsel of godly people as well as through more education, more training and other "legitimate" pursuits, but unhappiness overwhelmed me nonetheless.

And not only myself. I watched my efforts bring deeper frustration and greater disappointment as the issues of my life spilled over on the people I touched. Resentments, wrong attitudes, the hopelessness of one's "condition"— all may have negative effects on those closest to us. I spewed out my critical attitudes, distorted perspectives, wrong priorities and negative speaking on the people around me. In these ways I unintentionally "defiled" them.

Finally I understood. It was the first of many keys to change. *I accepted the reality that the power of God I needed for my breakthrough would be found in Christ alone.* I realized more and more that if I was ever going to experience significant change in my life, I must get to Jesus—and to Him alone. My destiny depended on it!

When we become reckless in our pursuit of Jesus, we become like this woman. When we are truly desperate, we will endure the misunderstanding of loved ones and the derision of the crowd in order to pursue our hope of finding wholeness and destiny in His presence.

I am grateful that Jesus did not condemn the woman who touched His garment that day. Instead, He commended the faith that had drawn virtue from Him. Likewise in our desperate attempts to touch Him, Jesus will minister grace to us, not the law of dos and don'ts. To receive a personal breakthrough from Jesus we must be willing to do as this woman did: Put all our hope in Him alone and press into Him. This act of faith is the beginning of all spiritual breakthroughs—to determine to touch Jesus Himself, the Lord of every breakthrough.

Note also that when this woman touched Jesus, not only was she restored to health herself but she was relieved of the fear of defiling others around her. Her breakthrough restored her personal health and her community life. When we press in and receive wholeness from the Lord, we can expect to be positive influences in the church community also. The Body of Christ has an incredible need for individuals to touch Jesus—to get our issues resolved so that we can function effectively as His Body in the earth.

Maybe you picked up this book because you need a personal breakthrough in your marriage or family. Maybe you are stuck in a job or relationship you do not like and you are looking for a way out. Maybe sickness, depression or financial problems plague you and you want to break out of those difficulties and discover the abundant life Jesus promised. Maybe you want to know where you "fit" in the Body of Christ. You are desperate to break through to your divine destiny and be effective in ministry. As you consider the keys to breakthrough we will discuss in these pages, please remember that the first principle for realizing dramatic change in our lives is to get to Jesus. Abandoning all other sources of help, determine to start there.

I had grown weary of trying to experience breakthroughs in my own strength. I regret the ceaseless, meaningless hours I spent trying to "fix" whatever problems surfaced— family crises, church problems, financial difficulties—

through my own exhausting efforts and limited understanding.

What the Holy Spirit is teaching me regarding touching Jesus has helped me to turn my focus from my "issues" and to humble myself in sheer abandon at His feet. In that place I have discovered the divine power I need to *break out* of the limitations of each situation and to *break through* into God's divine purposes.

Of course, life keeps happening. We have to remember in each new situation what we learned in the previous ones—how to focus on Him and get to His feet if we expect to be victorious. He does not give the same remedy for every situation, but He does give us direction. We must learn to be led by the Spirit as we wait on Him.

In addition, we need to understand that we have formidable enemies at work to keep us from changing. As we learn to identify the evil forces that are determined to keep us from walking in victory, we will also learn how to use the keys that God has given us to defeat them. Christ gained our victory for us at Calvary. It is up to us to appropriate it as we learn to walk in His power over the enemy.

— PRAYER —

Lord, today I purpose in my heart to press in and touch You in a new way. It is my deep desire to break through into Your purposes for my life. I realize that the most important change that must happen is in me. I ask You to open my understanding to Your ways as I pursue my breakthrough. Amen.

TWO

ENEMIES OF CHANGE

"Blessed be the Lord God of Israel, for He has visited us and accomplished redemption for His people ... Salvation from our enemies. ..."

LUKE 1 :68, 71

How many times have you sincerely pursued God's presence and power for your personal breakthrough, only to discover that forces are resisting you? Perhaps you felt defeated without understanding why or you were unable to pinpoint the reason for your frustration. It is important to understand that enemies are at work keeping you from making the changes you want to make.

The Bible teaches that one of our greatest enemies is Satan, the devil. This enemy is at work in the spiritual realm, and he is determined to keep you from touching Jesus. When we set out diligently to pursue the call and purposes of God for our lives, the devil sets out to oppose us with his fiendish strategies. He is threatened by the inevitable increase of the Kingdom of God when God's people discover their identities in Christ and begin to fulfill their personal destinies. His goal is to thwart us.

Dr. Sue Curran teaches that, according to the Scriptures, the devil works against God's people in three main ways: to tempt us, to deceive us and to accuse us.[1] The Bible clearly demonstrates the devil's attempts to defeat the people of God by these measures. Examples of both Old and New Testament saints show us how determined the devil is. King David, whom Scripture describes as a man after God's heart (see Acts 13:22), is a classic example. Though David's enemies appear to be other men, they were energized by the archenemy of all of God's purposes, Satan himself.

It is through David's experiences that we discern a key for victory. Then we will see how to use that key against two prevalent and powerful enemies that might surprise you.

DAVID FACES THE ENEMY

David first received his call and anointing as king over Israel when Samuel the prophet visited his family home and chose David from among his brothers. He did not receive that anointing with a big celebration and a public announcement. It was done secretly; it would have been dangerous to publicize the fact that a new king had been anointed for fear the reigning King Saul would try to destroy him.

Not only were the surroundings for David's anointing ordinary, done at home with his family, it also appears that David was a very ordinary young man. The prophet himself did not recognize David as God's choice. He thought that Eliab, the eldest brother, had the appearance of a future king. God had to speak to Samuel to tell him this was not the man. "Do not look at his appearance or at the height of his stature, because I have rejected him; for God sees not as man sees, for man looks at the outward appearance, but the LORD looks at the heart" (1 Samuel 16:7).

One by one the brothers were brought before Samuel and each was rejected as God's choice. When God did not indicate that he anoint any of these, Samuel asked Jesse, their father, if possibly there was another son. He replied that the youngest, David, was out tending the sheep. They sent for him in the pasture. When David was brought before Samuel, the Lord said, "Arise, anoint him; for this is he" (1 Samuel 16:12).

God had not chosen the firstborn, the mighty or the important according to the culture of the day. He chose instead the youngest son of Jesse who had not even been invited to dinner. Though the circumstances of his anointing were not extraordinary, the results were. The Scriptures declare that after his anointing, "the Spirit of the LORD came mightily upon David from that day forward" (1 Samuel 16:13).

Though David's anointing was verified by the presence and power of the Holy Spirit upon him, many years would pass before the purpose of that anointing would be fulfilled. He would experience painful and desperate circumstances before he would be crowned king over Israel. David had to learn how to defeat many different kinds of enemies that threatened to destroy him. Rather than destroy him, however, these difficult and perplexing situations prepared him for the rulership for which he was destined. They required he learn to seek God's plan for victory in each situation.

Even after David became king, when his anointing became an actual appointment, he continued to battle the enemies of God. The Scriptures tell us, for instance, that the Philistines "went up to seek out David" (2 Samuel 5:17). These pagan people were enemies of the one true God and tried on many occasions to destroy God's people. They represent a type or picture of the devil whose greatest desire is to destroy God's anointed. As David's anointing and authority increased, he became a greater threat to his enemies.

In our lives, as well, as we are pursuing the purposes of God, breaking through to places of greater anointing and authority in Him, we become a greater threat to the realms of darkness. Even though David had won victories against the Philistines previously, they still persisted in coming against him. Through tempting us to give up or accusing us falsely or trying to deceive us in some way, our enemy the devil will continue to wage war against our souls. What was David's secret to victory for each battle? Each time the Philistines came up against him, the Scriptures declare, "He inquired of the Lord."

> When the Philistines heard that they had anointed David king over Israel, all the Philistines went up to seek out David; and when David heard of it, he went down to the stronghold. Now the Philistines came and spread themselves out in the Valley of Rephaim. Then David *inquired of the LORD,* saying, "Shall I go up against the Philistines? Will You give them into my hand?" And the LORD said to David, "Go up, for I will certainly give the Philistines into your hand." So David came to Baal-perazim and defeated them there; and he said, "The LORD has broken through my enemies before me like the breakthrough of waters." Therefore he named that place Baal-perazim.
>
> 2 SAMUEL 5:17–20, EMPHASIS ADDED

Much as the woman with the issue of blood pressed in to touch Jesus for her breakthrough for healing, David pressed in to God to discover the winning strategy over his enemies. After his victory over the Philistines, David declared triumphantly, "The LORD has broken through my enemies before me like the breakthrough of waters" (verse 20). That place of the victory was then named Baal-perazim, which means "Master of the Breakthrough." Thus, David had discovered a principle for breakthrough in God, which is our next key to change: *God responds to His people to accomplish His purposes if they will come to Him and seek His strategy for the breakthrough they need.* He will fight our enemies and destroy them for us so we can gain the victory.

David also learned that he had to seek the Lord to maintain the victory he had gained. In the very same valley where David first defeated the Philistines, they made another raid against him. David did not assume that he was to win another victory in exactly the same way as he had won the previous one. Again, he inquired of the Lord for His strategy. He did not lean on his past experience but inquired of God to receive what was needed for the present battle. We, as well, must learn to gain fresh insight and revelation from the Lord for each battle if we, like David, are to maintain victory over Satan's relentless attacks.

David did not always walk in this principle of seeking God first, and when he did not, he experienced painful defeat. For example, after David became king of all of Israel, he determined to restore the presence of the Lord to them. You recall that the presence of the Lord dwelt in the Ark of the Covenant. Many years before David became king, because of Israel's disobedience, the Ark of the Covenant had been captured in battle. King Saul had never sought to have the presence of God restored to Israel. It was King David who desired the presence of God and determined to bring back the Ark of the Covenant.

In his first attempt to restore the Ark of the Covenant to Israel, David did not seek the Lord for His instruction (see 1 Chronicles 13). He decided that the Ark would be placed on a cart pulled by oxen. Fearing that it might fall off the cart, Uzzah reached out to steady it and he was struck dead. It was unlawful both to carry the Ark on a cart and to touch the presence of God. David became angry and fearful. Then he sought the Lord and studied the Scriptures to find God's direction.

He had learned a hard lesson. As Christians, we need to understand that it is not enough to desire the presence of the Lord for our personal lives or our churches. We must also seek God to find His ways that will release His presence.

When David gave the people instructions from the Word of God, they brought back the Ark. There was great rejoicing in Israel as God's presence once again dwelt with them. We must always press into God and seek Him according to His revealed will in Scripture. In our personal battles, God will always give us His strategy to defeat the devil. We must never presume that we can defeat him in our own strength, but must humble ourselves before God and seek Him in every situation. Then we will surely be victorious over this spiritual enemy in all of his attempts to defeat us.

OUR NATURAL ENEMY: THE WORLD

Once we know how the devil works against God's people, it becomes easier with prayer and diligence to recognize his blatant attempts to hinder us. There is another enemy that is not always so obvious, however, because it is such an integral part of our lives. It is as close as the surroundings and influences in life: It is what we call the natural world.

The natural world becomes an enemy when we focus too much on the cares of daily life. Many times these worries hide in legitimate situations. Marital problems, financial crises, health issues, etc. cannot simply be ignored. Similarly, the natural world becomes an enemy when we set our affections on it too highly. Jesus warned us that love of the world and its riches will have a powerful impact on us.

Let's see how the natural world can become an enemy of change.

The Cares of Life

Jesus taught us the danger of becoming embroiled in the worries of life. He said in His parable of the sower, "The seed cast in the weeds is the person who hears kingdom news, but weeds of worry, and illusions about getting more and wanting everything under the sun strangle what was heard and nothing comes of it" (Matthew 13:22, MESSAGE).

His meaning is clear. If we turn our eyes away from the Lord and onto our "issues," the weeds of worry will strangle the Word we need or the strategy we need for a breakthrough victory. We will not be able to hear the direction of the Lord because our problem has now become our enemy. It is our enemy because it stands in our way of touching the Lord. It has become bigger to us than God. Our vision is blocked and the breakthrough seems hopeless.

Instead of allowing the problem to consume us, we need to pursue God's presence in order to gain His perspective and directive. We put the principles of change into action when we do not allow our problems to become the focus of our lives, absorbing all our energies. Rather, we must allow them to be a catalyst for our abandonment to Jesus in order to receive a divine breakthrough—a God answer—for the situation.

In the early years of our marriage my husband and I faced difficult financial struggles. Dan had been laid off from his job and I had just found out that I was pregnant with our first child. I worried and cried and wondered, "How are we going to make it?"

Finally, I realized that I did not have the solution and, in my desperation, turned my eyes off of the problem and began to seek the presence of the Lord. While I was worshiping quietly one morning, I heard the Holy Spirit say, *Call your mortgage company and ask about your impound account.*

I did not even know what an impound account was, but I obeyed. I called the mortgage company and asked the clerk to check the balance in our impound account. She did so and informed me that we had an "overage." She said she would send us a check immediately and apologized for the oversight. That money was more than enough to meet our need. God's supply had been stored up for that time of financial crisis. As soon as I reached toward God, obeying His Word to cast my care on Him, the breakthrough came! He gave me clear instructions to follow to receive the financial answer we needed.

Before that breakthrough, the season of financial insecurity had become an enemy to my worship of God. The worry was robbing me of the sense of His presence. As I gave up the worry and worshiped Him, God's presence broke through against my enemy. I was able to hear His voice whispering the answer to my trouble. How we rejoiced at that unexpected provision! We, like David, could say, "The Lord has broken through . . . like the breakthrough of waters" (2 Samuel 5:20). A flood of joy and relief filled my heart as the Lord's presence confronted the problem and broke through our enemy of financial need.

Love of the World

Not only are the worries and cares of the world enemies of personal breakthrough, the love of the world also blocks the will of God from coming to us. Love for the world is a formidable enemy to the changes we need in our lives. The apostle John wrote, "Do not love the world nor the things in the world. If anyone loves the world, the love of the Father is not in him" (1 John 2:15). This issue speaks to the priorities of our affections. It addresses the matter of our emotional attachments to things and people, places and activities, even positions or accomplishments that have too important a place in our lives.

Jesus said, "Where your treasure is, there your heart will be also" (Matthew 6:21). If we value our "stuff"—possessions, positions and passions—above the provision of His presence, these things have become enemies of change. They have become our goals, our proofs of success. These "treasures" have successfully masqueraded as worthy ambitions for our fulfillment and satisfaction. They counterfeit our divine destiny and dull our desire to pursue God's presence and fulfill His purposes.

Countless people achieve goals and gain success by the world's standards. In doing so, they may never enjoy the victory of breakthrough in the realm of their God-ordained destiny. Then they wonder why they have not found the fulfillment they seek. Because the love of the world may overtake us in subtle ways, it is often difficult to recognize this destructive enemy.

When the rich young ruler questioned Jesus about eternal life, Jesus revealed to him what stood in the way of breakthrough to his personal destiny—his worldly riches. Jesus said, "Go and sell your possessions and give to the poor" (Matthew 19:21). This young man was not willing to leave the things his heart was attached to, so he went away sorrowful.

Jesus will help each of us discover the things in our lives that hinder us from fulfilling our divine purposes. When we ask Him to do that, however, we must be willing to hear Him and obey what He says to do. It is not that Jesus wants us to live without "things"; in Matthew 6:33 He promises that if we seek *first* God's Kingdom and His righteousness, all of these things will be added to us! Jesus promises to give us abundant life (see John 10:10), but we cannot experience His abundance if we are pursuing our own interests apart from His will.

Discovering our personal destinies in God will include the things He knows will bring us ultimate good, the people He knows will give us greatest fulfillment and the place of ministry He knows will most satisfy us. He wants us to break through into His presence to receive all that He has determined as a part of our eternal destiny! Only then will possessions, people and positions take their proper places in our lives.

Why not stop here and invite the Holy Spirit to do a heart check? Ask yourself: "What or whom do I think about the most? What occupies most of my time? What is my favorite topic of conversation?" Ask the Holy Spirit to reveal to you the priorities of your affections, the emotional attachments that govern your life. If your response to these questions is *anything* or *anyone* other than the Lord and the pursuit of His purposes and desires, you will have identified an enemy to your personal breakthrough to divine destiny.

OUR PERSONAL ENEMY: THE FLESH

We have discussed briefly the devil and the natural world as enemies of our breakthrough to divine destiny. Another powerful enemy that is even closer to us than these foes is our own "self." Self is perhaps the most difficult enemy to recognize and therefore the most dangerous and threatening to our personal breakthroughs. Even if our hearts are longing to follow God, and we learn to resist the tactics of the devil and escape the pull of the world, we still have to be aware of the strength of the self-nature to keep us from God's purposes for our lives. Scripture makes it clear that the self-life is opposed to the purposeful life God wants to develop within us.

Just look at some of the deeds of the flesh listed by the apostle Paul in Galatians 5:19–21: immorality, impurity, sensuality, idolatry, sorcery, enmities, strife, jealousy, outbursts of anger, disputes, dissensions, factions, envying, drunkenness and carousing. It is no wonder that the Old Testament prophet Jeremiah declared that the heart of a man is deceitful and wicked above all else! "Who can understand it?" (Jeremiah 17:9).

Paul stated further:

> A natural man does not accept the things of the Spirit of God, for they are foolishness to him; and he cannot understand them, because they are spiritually appraised.
>
> 1 CORINTHIANS 2:14

The way that we are inclined to respond is actually the opposite of the way God would want us to respond. Because of the sinful state of fallen man, our natural thinking cannot be trusted.

Paul also described the natural mind as being hostile to God (see Romans 7). We are familiar with the cliché "He is his own worst enemy." According to the Scriptures, this is truer than we realize. We may think, *How can this be? After all, I know me—at least I think I do! I know my weaknesses and strengths, likes and dislikes, goals and ambitions—and secret desires. Don't I?* Probably not as well as we think. That is what makes the self-life such a formidable foe. Though I think I know myself, I must submit to the truth of Scripture that my heart deceives me and my natural mind thinks contrary to the will of God for me.

To help us conquer this enemy, Paul urged Christians to surrender to the Lordship of Christ. He declared:

> Therefore I urge you, brethren, by the mercies of God, to present your bodies a living and holy sacrifice, acceptable to God, which is your spiritual service of worship. And do not be conformed to this world, but be transformed by the renewing of your mind, so that you may prove what the will of God is, that which is good and acceptable and perfect.
>
> ROMANS 12:1–2

I cannot know the deceitfulness of my heart, and yet the Scriptures declare that God desires truth in the innermost being (see Psalm 51:6). What is the answer to my dilemma? Until we have the inner witness of the Holy Spirit, we are not really capable of knowing ourselves. I need divine help to conquer this enemy of self. God in His mercy has provided that help for me. The writer of Hebrews declares:

> For the word of God is living and active and sharper than any two-edged sword, and piercing as far as the division of soul and spirit, of both joints and marrow, and able to judge

the thoughts and intentions of the heart. And there is no creature hidden from His sight, but all things are open and laid bare to the eyes of Him with whom we have to do.

HEBREWS 4:12–13

God's Word is powerful as a two-edged sword that penetrates and divides between my soul or self-life and my spirit. As I study the Word of God, the truth it reveals may wound me. It will expose my wrong thinking, my misplaced affections and my misguided choices. When I experience the light of the Word shining in the darkness of my soul, that is not the time to justify myself or make excuses. Rather it is a time to repent for the sin in my self-life that has been revealed.

One of my most excruciating battles with this enemy of self occurred in a meeting at a conference I attended. A well-known minister was speaking from the biblical account of Elisha asking the prophet Elijah for a double portion of the anointing of God he saw working in Elijah's life. The minister finished her message that day, and began walking back and forth and praying for a double portion to be released to us. She stopped directly in front of me, laid her hands on my head and said, "Lord, let a double portion of the anointing You have placed on my life be upon her." I was so excited! I had long had a secret desire to receive a prayer of impartation from this great woman of God.

At the end of the session, I headed for my hotel room. I was floating on air. I felt so significant and honored, so special. I congratulated myself that I was the *only* one she had prayed for in that way. By the time I got to my room my head was so big from my exalting thoughts that it could hardly fit through the door!

As I continued with these self-elevating thoughts, suddenly I felt the awesome presence of the Lord fill that hotel room. An overwhelming fear of the Lord filled my heart. I fell to the floor—facedown. Minutes before, in my self-indulging exaltation, I was "flying high." Now, as I lay prostrate before the awesome presence of God, it seemed I could not get low enough. In His presence, I began to realize the awfulness of my pride. And I was afraid. The brightness of His presence had uncovered the true condition of the darkness of my heart.

As I lay there, the Lord spoke to me about my secret desire for a greater anointing. *Daughter, you have desired a good thing. But I can't trust you with it now.* I felt my heart break at His words. I began to sob. But I understood that the pride of my self-life was the enemy that was keeping me from my destiny. Out of the depths of my being, I heard myself cry, "Lord, have mercy. I am the woman. I am the woman." I repeated it over and over still weeping in His presence.

At that moment I realized that the dream I had experienced years earlier was not simply about my participating in the Bible account of the woman with the issue of blood, as I had thought. It was *my* story. God was revealing the issues of my heart. I was unclean. I realized that my pride had defiled many as I touched their lives in "ministry." On that day, I made a promise that I would never again touch His people (even in well-meaning attempts to minister to them) without allowing Him to cleanse me first. As I am cleansed of my issues He can touch others through me with His touch—not mine; His ministry to them will heal—not mine. I surrendered to Him in that fearful, wonderful place of self-revelation.

Of course, to gain victory over all our enemies requires that we allow the Holy Spirit continually to reveal the darkness of our minds and hearts, and repent for whatever He reveals. Complete victory requires a process—it is not accomplished in an instant. As I purpose to touch the Lord daily, allowing His Word to wash me, I experience a fresh encounter with Calvary and the power of Christ's blood to cleanse me and give me personal victory. At the cross, my flesh—my worst enemy—continually loses its power to rule in my life. This is one of the most powerful components of personal breakthrough I have learned—defeating self by bringing it to the cross.

In choosing to humble myself in deep contrition of heart and through repentance, I experience victory over this hidden enemy of self. Only in the light of God's Word, being willing to see His truth about me, can the secret darkness and deception of my heart be exposed to reveal my true spiritual condition. In that place of painful revelation, as I cry out to God, He will cleanse me and change me, defeating this dangerous enemy that threatens to keep me from my personal breakthrough in God.

Jesus said, "You will know the truth, and the truth will make you free" (John 8:32). It is the truth of God's Word that has the power to set us free from ourselves! As we allow this cleansing work to be done in our lives, the victorious life of Christ will triumph in our hearts. Then we can say with Paul the apostle: "I have been crucified with Christ; and it is no longer I who live, but Christ lives in me; and the life which I now live in the flesh I live by the faith in the Son of God, who loved me and gave Himself up for me" (Galatians 2:20). The more I allow the life of Christ to increase in my life, the less room there is for my destructive self-life.

Scripture is clear that there is a war raging within us! "For the flesh [the *self-life*] sets its desire against the Spirit, and the Spirit against the flesh; for these are in opposition to one another, so that you may not do the things that you please" (Galatians 5:17). Even the great apostle Paul said of his own conflict: "For what I am doing, I do not understand; for I am not practicing what I would like to do, but I am doing the very thing I hate" (Romans 7:15).

Have you ever felt this way? Have you been frustrated with your own flesh and nature? Your carnal thoughts, wrong attitudes, negative speaking? If we allow that frustration to bring us to a state of desperation for change and set ourselves to seek the Lord with all of our hearts, it will work for our good. The result of our seeking will be a healthy dependence on the Lord.

Quoting Psalm 95, the writer to the Hebrews admonished: "Today if you hear His voice, do not harden your hearts" (Hebrews 4:7). As we determine to seek the Lord for personal breakthrough, the voice of the Lord comes to lead us to the cross. There we must die to our own ways and receive His divine nature in exchange for the self-life. This is what Jesus meant when He said that His disciples must daily deny themselves, take up their crosses and follow Him (see Matthew 16:24). Victory over the enemy of self is only gained at Calvary. We must deny the "rights" to our wills, our thoughts and our emotions, and surrender to His will, thoughts and emotions for us. That is how to take up the cross and follow Him victoriously.

As I give myself to the study of God's Word and pursue the reality of His presence in my life, I move closer to my breakthrough for personal revival and divine destiny. I find my self-life crowded out by His wonderful presence.

The Scriptures reveal to us all that we need to fulfill our destinies in God. As we determine to pursue our personal breakthroughs, coming to God and seeking His strategies for us, we will encounter the enemies of the world, the flesh and the devil. But we will also achieve victory in each situation as we become sensitive to the Holy Spirit and allow Him to cleanse us from all unrighteousness.

We should not fear these enemies, for God has promised us victory as we submit to Him. May we never harden our hearts to the Holy Spirit's conviction.

— PRAYER —

Lord, please shine Your light on my heart and reveal the enemies of my breakthrough. I realize that my heart is deceitful and I need Your truth to penetrate any places of darkness. Show me Your strategy for each situation as I inquire of You. Teach me, Holy Spirit, how to take up my cross and follow Jesus. I know that in that place, I will experience fulfillment and victory. Amen.

THREE

DIVINE
DISSATISFACTION

As the deer pants for the water brooks, so my soul pants for You, O God.

PSALM 42:1

The world of technology, whether medical, scientific, archeological, electronic or some other field, is constantly competing to achieve new breakthroughs. Experts in these fields must be willing to leave what has "worked" in the past in order to pursue what is needed for the future. Skeletons of once powerful companies that were lax in the area of research and development dot the business horizon as stark reminders of their failure to pursue breakthroughs in their particular fields of technology.

NO CAMPING!

The need to pursue new breakthroughs is no less imperative for the Church and for individual Christians than it is for the world of technology. We must determine to progress in our knowledge of God and in developing a relationship with Him in order to survive destruction from our enemies, as we have discussed. Most of us can bring to mind at least one person who seemed to be a strong, mature Christian, perhaps even a pastor or leader, whose life was destroyed because he or she did not survive the onslaught of one or more of these enemies.

In order to experience a spiritual breakthrough, we must be willing to leave behind what has "worked" for us in the past. It may not be what we need to face the present and future challenges. The prophet Elijah must have enjoyed receiving food supernaturally from the ravens as he hid from the wrath of the king to whom he had prophesied the present famine. But when the brook dried up and the ravens did not come any longer, he had to be willing for a change in lifestyle and a fresh word from God so that he could continue to survive.

Many Christians receive supernatural blessings from God as Elijah did, and "camp" there, thinking that is all they need for the rest of their lives. They do not realize that the supply of life has dried up and God wants to do something new for them. They only sense that they are weary of traveling in the same cycle and are struck to the core of their being with a sense of dissatisfaction.

In a word, they—we—need revival.

In the Scriptures, brass heavens and barren land are pictures of our depleted spiritual condition, individually and corporately. We wonder why our prayers seem to go no higher than the ceilings of our churches. We have poorly attended prayer meetings with little evidence of fruitfulness. We have worship services that are void of God's presence and power.

John Kilpatrick, pastor of Brownsville Assembly of God in Pensacola, Florida, has experienced five years of continual revival with up to 180,000 souls saved. He states, "Revival cannot come until the heavens are made crystal clear through repentance and prayer. Revival will not come until God's people allow themselves to be changed and prepared through the discipline of fervent prayer."[1]

Thus, we discover our next key to change: *If we humble ourselves before God and cry out to be delivered from our desolation, we will find ourselves on a breakthrough journey into His presence where our relationship with God will be enlarged and our prayers will be answered.*

A PROPHETIC PICTURE: NAOMI RETURNS HOME

We see in the historical narrative of the book of Ruth in the Old Testament a prophetic picture of the Church. This book was written in the days of the judges when "everyone did what was right in his own eyes" (Judges 21:25). God's judgment against this rampant independence from His appointed authority brought famine to the land of Bethlehem. In the Hebrew language, *Bethlehem* means "house of bread." Sin had robbed this fruitful land of its divine purpose.

The famine drove a man named Elimelech and his family into the foreign, pagan land of Moab. Dwelling there in that land of idolatry, Elimelech and Naomi raised their two sons and allowed them to marry two Moabite girls. After several years, Elimelech and his two sons died. This tragedy must have broken Naomi's heart, as well as leaving her, a widow, to fight for survival in a culture that did not support women who were alone.

Then Naomi heard that the Lord had visited His people and given them food—bread was once again in Bethlehem. When she heard this, her immediate response was to "[depart] from the place she was" (Ruth 1:7) and return to her homeland. Her "divine dissatisfaction" would lead her to break through to her destiny.

Naomi's daughter-in-law, Ruth, was also desperate for a breakthrough. This Moabite girl could have returned to her parents' household, but she was determined to seek the living God and forsake her idolatrous past. Ruth would not part from the woman who would lead her ultimately to her own divine destiny. Her poignant cry determined her release into God's purposes for her life:

> But Ruth said, "Do not urge me to leave you or turn back from following you; for where you go, I will go, and where you lodge, I will lodge. Your people shall be my people, and your God, my God. Where you die, I will die, and there I will be buried. Thus may the Lord do to me, and worse, if anything but death parts you and me."
>
> RUTH 1:16–17

Naomi's God had become more important to Ruth than all that was familiar, than family, than life itself. So Ruth accompanied her mother-in-law as they returned to the "house of bread" (Bethlehem) never dreaming of the breakthrough that the Lord would provide through their kinsman Boaz.

Drawn to the Source

Just as Naomi and Ruth returned to their homeland and received the divine destiny awaiting them, so the Church has experienced a desperate famine and is beginning to receive news that there is bread at home.

Perhaps you, like Naomi, find yourself in a crisis that might be described as a sense of emptiness and dryness, a famine of the soul. It makes you feel desperate for a change—a spiritual breakthrough. You may feel heartbroken over life's situations or just homesick for God. A broken heart pulls us to God and God to us like a magnet. Can you feel the pull of His presence in your pain?

In Naomi's heartbreak, she was drawn back to the source of former joys. God promises to come near to the broken-hearted. The psalmist declared: "The LORD is near to the brokenhearted and saves those who are crushed in spirit" (Psalm 34:18). In another place, the Scriptures teach us: "Draw near to God and He will draw near to you" (James 4:8). Maybe the longing in your heart is the Lord drawing you back to Himself, your Source of joy. Possibly, you are aching for what "used to be" in your relationship with Him. Sometimes it takes a crisis or heartbreak in our lives to cause us to realize that we need to return "home." In one of his desperate moments, the psalmist said:

> As the deer pants for the water brooks, so my soul pants for You, O God. My soul thirsts for God, for the living God; when shall I come and appear before God? My tears have been my food day and night, while they say to me all day long, "Where is your God?" These things I remember and I pour out my soul within me. For I used to go along with the throng and lead them in procession to the house of God, with the voice of joy and thanksgiving, a multitude keeping festival.
>
> PSALM 42:1–4

He, like Naomi, discovered that true joy is only found at "home"—in the presence of the Lord.

As God draws near to us, giving us the message of hope that there is food in the "house of bread," we must choose, like Naomi and Ruth, to depart from the place where we are now, and move in the direction of His presence and provision. And we can expect the provision of God to surprise us as much as the wondrous provision Naomi and Ruth ultimately received must have surprised them. When they returned home, they had no idea what their future would be. All they knew was that the famine was over in the land of their God, and they would be able to satisfy their hunger.

The Ripple Effect

The first surprise that awaited Naomi and Ruth was the impact their return had on the people of the city. As they arrived in Bethlehem, "all the city was stirred because of them" (Ruth 1:19). We may expect to have an impact on the lives around us also as we turn our hearts to seek God and pursue personal breakthrough, returning "home" to Jesus—our house of bread. As entire churches choose to seek God's fresh provision, we can expect our cities to be stirred. Those living around us will be affected as they watch the purposes of God being manifested in our lives, individually and corporately.

I believe it is significant that Naomi and Ruth arrived in Bethlehem in the beginning of the early harvest of barley (see 1:22). This natural harvest of grain is a picture of the spiritual harvest of souls that is awaiting the Church's return to a passionate pursuit of the Lord. It is imperative to the impending harvest of souls that we return to our God, wholeheartedly seeking His purposes for our lives. Though they may not have been aware of it, Naomi and Ruth had positioned themselves on the threshold of personal breakthrough for their divine destinies. Is it possible that the same is true of you? Could it be that the change you so desire is closer than you think?

A New Identity

Boaz, a near kinsman to Naomi who would redeem these widows from their poverty, was living in Bethlehem. (Women had homes in that culture only if they were related to men. It was the responsibility of brothers of the deceased or other close kin to marry widows so that they would have a source of income, shelter and protection.)

This wealthy man, whose name means "in him is strength," became captivated by the young Moabite woman who gleaned grain from his fields to provide food for herself and her mother-in-law. When Naomi instructed Ruth in the proper way to get to the feet of Boaz, Ruth followed her instructions and made her request to Boaz to redeem her. He was deeply touched by her kindness and did all that was necessary to redeem Naomi, including making Ruth his wife. So Naomi was restored to her inheritance and Ruth shared not only the wealth of Boaz, but his life as well.

Prophetically, Boaz represents Christ and His relationship to the Church. We, like Ruth, are foreigners and total strangers to God. Christ has pity on our poverty of sin and offers to redeem us, giving us the eternal inheritance of His divine wealth. Not only do we share His divine riches, but His life as well. Shamelessly, Christ changes our identities and brings us into His royal family.

Ruth's identity was completely changed. No longer a "Moabite gleaner," she was now the wife of a notable man in the community. She had chosen to forsake her idols and follow the one true God of Naomi, and had been rewarded by great temporal blessings and honor besides. And because of the life she shared with Boaz, she gave birth to a son, Obed. The Scriptures declare that Obed was the great-grandfather of King David. That placed Ruth in the lineage of David and sealed her in the lineage of Christ forever. What an eternal destiny Ruth's response to God in her personal crisis had unfolded! She could look back from her place of blessing and see that her great affliction had become her friend. The psalmist had this understanding when he declared: "It is good for me that I was afflicted, that I may learn Your statutes" (Psalm 119:71).

REVIVAL RAIN AND TEARS THAT COUNT

I remember a time of spiritual crisis in my life when I felt there was a famine in my heart, a sense of desperation, for the presence of God. Difficult life situations had caused this sense of desperation in me. The Holy Spirit used my affliction to cause me to seek God. I knew that I needed a personal revival of love for God. Only then would I find relief from the pain in my heart. I asked the Lord, "Where does the rain for revival come from?" He answered my question with a question of His own: *What causes you to weep?* As I pondered His question, the Holy Spirit began to turn back the pages of my memories.

I remembered times when I had wept bitterly over what my mother used to call "spilt milk." I wept over situations in my life that I despised and that were painfully unchangeable. As the Holy Spirit reviewed with me the history of my tears, I discovered that many times my tears were caused by regret and remorse. And I revisited several "pity parties" where I had indulged myself in feelings of self-justification and resentment toward others.

I understood what the Lord was trying to show me: Rain for revival is made of tears—the right kind of tears. Because my tears were tears of bitterness and self-pity caused by my disappointment, disillusionment and discouragement, they had not produced revival rain in my heart. They were a result of focusing on my feelings instead of relating to the loving heart of God and His desires for me and for others. This wrong focus had caused a famine in my heart for the presence of God.

I was reminded of God's promise that if we will "weep between the porch and the altar," we will gain the fruitfulness of the harvest (see Joel 2:17–19). If we will stretch ourselves out between lost souls and the cross and cry out to God, He will heal our land. He will come to us "like the rain, like the spring rain watering the earth" (Hosea 6:3). The psalmist promises that if we will sow with tears, we will reap with joy (see Psalm 126:5).

Suddenly, as the Spirit opened my understanding, my heart began to break over my condition. I wanted my tears to count. I wept in deep sorrow and repentance for my self-focused way of living. As I dropped my own burden of emotional care in that place of prayer, I picked up His. He caused me to share in His sufferings for hurting humanity and allowed my heart to be joined to His (see Philippians 3:10). At that moment I touched my personal destiny in God and experienced a breakthrough into the purposes of God for my life.

The tears the Holy Spirit had produced in me had turned to revival rain for my life, healing my heart and allowing me to touch the heart of God. It is God's desire to bring us "home" to His purposes for our lives. The stirring of dissatisfaction in our hearts is the starting point for our personal breakthrough. Though the circumstances of our lives may be natural, the source of this discontent is divine. It is God's way of bringing us to a place of making right choices to seek Him.

Sometimes when we feel this discontentment, we are tempted to fill our emptiness with other things. If the crisis of spiritual famine has not left you with a sense of hunger for God, maybe you have found other ways to satisfy the cravings of your soul. In *The God Catchers*, Tommy Tenney states:

> Our problem is our diet. We like to stuff ourselves on spiritual junk food and feast on dainty bless-me treats. That is the kind of spiritual "food" that has all the form and outward appearance of godliness, but is a standing denial of its power.[2]

My four-year-old granddaughter, Meshea, loves to come to our house, especially for the treats! If we let her (and usually we do) she fills her little tummy with marshmallows, chocolate kisses and Cheetos! When it is time for dinner, she has no appetite for "real" food. Her appetite was ruined by the junk food. If this was allowed on a daily basis with no other nourishment, she would eventually get sick and even possibly die of malnutrition! Even though her tummy feels full, she really has not had her needs met.

This is what happens to us spiritually when we insist on a quick fix of spiritual fast food. We find a preacher or a ministry somewhere that makes us feel better somehow. Maybe our discomfort is relieved by a prophecy or a prayer about how wonderful we are and how blessed we will be. Or we buy the latest worship CD that has the latest song and we get goose bumps and feel spiritual for a while. I am not opposed to preachers or prophecies that encourage and build up God's people and I have stacks of worship CDs, but I have found the *best* of these will not satisfy the craving for the Bread of His Presence.

If spiritual fast food does not work, we might be tempted to fill up on spiritual activities. We busy ourselves with religious programs and events to avoid coming face to face with our condition—our deep need for him, the Bread of Life. These things will satisfy us temporarily, but then the gnawing hunger pangs will begin again.

Do you agree with me that it is time for change? Why not, like Naomi and Ruth, get up and follow your hunger to the "house of bread"? Satisfaction and surprises await you!

— PRAYER —

Father, I am hungry and thirsty. The famine I feel for You, the Word of Life, has left me desperate and discontent. Forgive me for filling my empty soul with other "foods," activities and relationships. So many times I have had my eyes on my problems instead of upon Your presence and purpose. I want to come home to my Source of joy. And when I do go through difficult times, please turn my tears into revival rain. Thank You for this starting point of personal breakthrough—my personal dissatisfaction. I choose to seek You and allow the Holy Spirit to reveal to me the things in my life that hinder my destiny in You from becoming a reality. Amen.

FOUR

GOD'S FAVOR

"Therefore repent and return, so that your sins may be wiped away, in order that times of refreshing may come from the presence of the Lord."

ACTS 3:19

A highway will be there, a roadway, and it will be called the Highway of Holiness. . . . And the ransomed of the LORD will return and come with joyful shouting to Zion, with everlasting joy upon their heads. They will find gladness and joy, and sorrow and sighing will flee away.

ISAIAH 35:8, 10

There was a time early in my Christian walk that if I heard the preacher say the word *repent*, I would brace myself for a "hell-fire and brimstone" sermon—one packed full of fear tactics and condemnation. I would be convinced by the fiery words that I was a very bad person with little or no chance of ever seeing heaven. Red-faced he would scream: "Repent!"

It was not until many years later that I became aware that the message of repentance is the love message of the Holy Spirit. It was at a time that my "divine dissatisfaction" had stirred me to seek God with all of my heart. I discovered that repentance was a fundamental principle for experiencing the presence of God in my life.

It was this simple message that John the Baptist preached in the wilderness of Judea to lead Israel back to God.

"Repent, for the kingdom of heaven is at hand" (Matthew 3:1). Isaiah called him "the voice of one crying in the wilderness, make ready the way of the LORD, make His paths straight" (Matthew 3:3). Today, the Holy Spirit cries out in the desert, dry places of our lives—those places that are barren and fruitless: "Come, this way. I will lead you out of this wilderness. Repent and receive the refreshing rain of God's presence." It is the love language of God who has made a pathway for us to come out of our present condition and come into His purposes. As His love conquers us, our hardened hearts begin to break.

It is true that even as the Holy Spirit brooded over the surface of the deep in the beginning (see Genesis 1:2), He hovers also over the darkness of our souls and draws us to Jesus. Just as the Word of God sent the power of light to scatter the darkness in the beginning of time, so the Holy Spirit reveals Jesus to us through His Word and draws us to repentance.

When the Holy Spirit shines His light into our hearts, we are drawn to answer the deep call of God's heart for unbroken fellowship and relationship with Him. If we continue to answer that call and cultivate an intimate relationship with God, our hearts will continue to break in deep repentance for our sin as the light of God shines into every darkened area of our souls.

The more we gaze upon Him, beholding His love, the more we are changed (see 2 Corinthians 3:18). *Brokenness followed by repentance results in obedience.* This is our next key. Let's look at each of these breakthrough concepts. Isn't it time for a change?

BROKENNESS—A HEART PREPARED

Brokenness is often the state of mind and heart that produces repentance. When we realize that our sins have separated us from the Lord, our hearts break to think that we have hurt Him and others. Quickly, the Holy Spirit directs us back to His presence and we repent. When I draw near to the Lord in worship, many times the Holy Spirit will whisper a convicting word to me. In the brilliance of His beauty, I join with the prophet Isaiah and cry, "Woe is me, for I am ruined! Because I am a man of unclean lips, and I live among a people of unclean lips; for my eyes have seen the King, the LORD of hosts" (Isaiah 6:5). There is something about standing before Him in His light that reveals the darkness of our own lives!

Other times I become aware of my condition in daily life activities when the Holy Spirit gently nudges me and brings to my attention that I am not behaving in a Christ-like manner. He has many times sweetly said to me, *That hurts My feelings.* My heart breaks and I rush to the altar of repentance.

Tommy Tenney teaches that "brokenness on earth creates openness in heaven."[1] The psalmist understood that "the LORD is near to the brokenhearted and saves those who are crushed in spirit" (Psalm 34:18). Again, the psalmist declared: "The sacrifices of God are a broken spirit; a broken and contrite heart, O God, You will not despise" (Psalm 51:17). In this poignant psalm that models repentance for us, we learn that brokenness of heart is what God desires as His dwelling place. Not only will we experience breakthrough to personal healing and revival in our brokenness of heart over our sins, but also we will begin to walk in a lifestyle of repentance.

REPENTANCE DEFINED

Repentance is much more than a simple apology to God for our behavior or attitudes. It is more than turning from sin and walking in the opposite direction. When a child is disciplined for inappropriate behavior, the behavior may change but the heart may remain the same. Most of us have heard the expression, "I may be sitting down, but I'm standing up on the inside!" Many times we do the "right" things because of the fear of the consequences, but our hearts are unchanged. When raising our daughters, Melanie and Kari, we would always insist that they say they were sorry and hug each other after one of their "spats." If they refused, they would be punished. So, begrudgingly, they would mutter, "Sorry," and barely give a hug.

One day—the girls were ten and six at the time—I was discussing this process with my friend Dr. Dianne McIntosh, a psychologist and counselor. She said to me, "Did they repent?"

I answered, "Yes, they said 'sorry.'"

She then wisely explained to me the difference between behavior modification and heart change. I learned that day that repentance is the result of revelation. Once the Holy Spirit reveals to us God's viewpoint and perspective, our hearts break over our actions and our minds change to His way of thinking. Then, our behavior will change to His way of doing things. Once I understood this principle, not only was my parenting revolutionized, but my own life was as well. From then on, whenever my girls fought I sent them to their rooms to ask the Holy Spirit what they needed to repent of. He was always faithful to reveal the truth to them! Then, as they embraced His word in the situation, they were able eventually to repent and embrace each other.[2]

The Greek word for *repentance* is *metanoia. Meta* means "after" and *noieo* means "to know."[3] A literal rendering of the Greek word for repentance then would be "a knowing after." Dutch Sheets states: "It [repentance] is a new knowledge, perception or understanding that comes to us 'after' our previous understanding. It is a change of mind."[4] He also states: "Revival is a process. God is into seasoned, well-baked and tender. He is not into instant or micro-waveable. And the process of revival begins with the process of repentance."[5]

Because the god of this world, Satan, has blinded our minds so that we cannot see the "light of the gospel of the glory of Christ" (2 Corinthians 4:4), we need a new perception or perspective so that our returning to God to walk in His ways will be possible. Once the Holy Spirit shines His light into our hearts and reveals the truth to us regarding our need for change, we can then reposition ourselves through a new repentance to align with the Lord and His ways. Dutch Sheets declares, "Anytime He [God] adjusts us to His way of thinking through a revelation of the Holy Spirit, which should happen regularly, this is repentance."[6]

TIMES OF REFRESHING

When Peter and John healed the lame man who sat at the gate of the Temple, the people who witnessed this miracle were astonished at such power. Peter took advantage of the opportunity to preach the Gospel to them, beginning with a brief account of how Jesus came to save them, and how they rejected Him and crucified Him. Then Peter instructed them: "Therefore repent and return, so that your sins may be wiped away, in order that times of refreshing may come from the presence of the Lord" (Acts 3:19).

If we read this verse with the literal meanings of the words in Greek we would understand it this way:

> *"Repent"*—that is, position yourself to be in right relationship—"therefore, and *return"*—that is, come back to the original place—"that your sins may be wiped away, in order that *times"*—*(kairos)* strategic moments, windows of opportunity—"of *refreshing"*—that is, a recovery of breath—"may come from the *presence"*— that is, the gaze of His countenance—"of the Lord."

Feeling lifeless and hopeless, in need of refreshing, can mean that we are living in a *kairos* time, a strategic moment of opportunity. If we turn to God in that moment, we can expect to "breathe again"—sensing a new strength of life and hope even in the midst of difficult circumstances. When Peter spoke the word *refreshing*, he was declaring to them that a new life in God awaited them. The life they had known according to their Jewish religion, culture and tradition could not satisfy their present need for God's presence. They must repent of their sins and accept Christ Jesus, the new and living Way, in order to experience the refreshing they needed.

We must learn to live daily in a heart attitude of repentance in order that the fresh breezes of God's presence can continually blow upon us.

Similarly, our church life as we know it, with all of its traditions and culture, can grow stale and lifeless without the refreshing that repentance brings. We can find ourselves simply going through the motions of religious activity as we slowly die within to any sense of destiny for our lives. Our dreams and visions begin to grow dim because of the blinding whirlwind created by our own busyness.

The message to us is the same one that Peter preached that day: Repent and return. "Come back to the original place of life and I will meet you there," is the promise of the Holy Spirit. When this is our daily experience with the Lord, we will be positioned to seize those *kairos* moments or windows of opportunity for new revelation and deeper repentance that will result in a new intimacy with God. When we live repentant lives, we will find ourselves walking consistently in the will of God. We will not miss the special moments that are God-ordained to unlock our destinies. To experience those moments is to be refreshed in God's presence. We will find ourselves supernaturally energized to accomplish what God has called us to do. Our lives will be free of regrets and we will enjoy the freedom that comes from true fulfillment.

Many times when I feel that God is far from me and I cannot sense His presence, I find that this is usually an indication of my need for fresh repentance. As I turn to seek the Lord and ask Him to search my heart and reveal any sin issues, He is faithful to show me where I grieved the Holy Spirit by a particular action, words or thoughts that I have been dwelling upon. When I repent of my sin, the presence of God is restored and I experience the joy of the Lord again.

Basilea Schlink, in her wonderful little book, *Repentance—The JOY-Filled Life*, writes:

Repentance—the gateway to heaven! Repentance—the gateway to the very heart of the Father! Repentance makes us joyful, for it brings us home to the Father, home to heaven. Repentance restores the presence of the Lord to our lives. When John the Baptist preached the message of repentance to the people of Israel in the wilderness, He was preparing them for the imminent coming of their Messiah. Israel had been void of the presence of God for over 400 years. The ark of the covenant had been carried into captivity and the Holy of Holies was just an empty room behind the veil. The wilderness where they heard John preach matched the wilderness of their souls that were arid and desperate to drink the life-giving waters of the presence of the Lord.[7]

As these Jewish people listened to John, they were convicted of their sins and entered into John's baptism of repentance. Their hearts were opened to recognize Christ as their Messiah. Isaiah prophesied of a day when Israel would see the glory of God:

Then the eyes of the blind will be opened and the ears of the deaf will be unstopped. Then the lame will leap like a deer, and the tongue of the mute will shout for joy. For waters will break forth in the wilderness and streams in the Arabah [desert]. The scorched land will become a pool and the thirsty ground springs of water.

ISAIAH 35:5–7

The breaking forth of waters is a beautiful picture of the life of God satiating the dry ground of the wilderness of our lives through our repentance. Hosea used this analogy for revival, declaring to those who return to the Lord and seek Him: "He will come to us like the rain, like the spring rain watering the earth" (Hosea 6:3). Though Jesus had no need of personal repentance, He responded to the baptism of repentance that John preached, identifying with us even in this act of obedience. As soon as He came out of the waters of baptism, the heavens opened and a Voice out of heaven spoke and said, "You are My beloved Son, in You I am well-pleased" (Mark 1:11).

Following His temptation by the devil in the wilderness, Jesus, full of the Spirit, began to preach and to work miracles—signs and wonders that set people free from their bondage. Through the ministry of Jesus, the refreshing, life-giving waters of God's presence had broken forth in the wilderness. And how did all of this begin? It began with the breakthrough message of John: "Repent, for the kingdom of heaven is at hand."

Jesus used the analogy of water to represent God's presence in a slightly different way, declaring, "'If any one is thirsty, let him come to Me and drink. He who believes in Me, as the Scripture said, 'From his innermost being will flow rivers of living water.'" But this He spoke of the Spirit" (John 7:37–39). In the wilderness of our lives, as we repent and bring our thirsty souls to Jesus, the waters of divine life, the presence of the Holy Spirit within us, will *break forth!* This will not only result in our personal deliverance and revival but also affect those around us. As we submit to His leadership, God will release His presence into our lives like a flood.

Again the prophet Isaiah declared this reality: "From the west, men will fear the name of the LORD, and from the rising of the sun, they will revere his glory. For he will come like a pent-up flood that the breath of the LORD drives along" (Isaiah 59:19, NIV). This vivid picture of floodwaters rushing along characterizes the power of God that will work through our lives as we reverence Him and allow Him to reign. We can then begin to identify with the sins of our families, regions and nations. We can be a part of bringing healing for our land (see 2 Chronicles 7:14).

GETTING GOD'S ATTENTION

Where do we start in our quest for heartfelt brokenness and true repentance?

Let's look at the example of the prophet Daniel. He set himself to fast, pray and repent for the sins of his people, and he received an angelic visitation in response to his cry of repentance:

> Now while I was speaking and praying, and confessing my sin and the sin of my people Israel, and presenting my supplication before the Lord my God in behalf of the holy mountain of my God, while I was still speaking in prayer, then the man Gabriel, whom I had seen in the vision previously, came to me in my extreme weariness about the time of the evening offering.
>
> DANIEL 9:20–21

Daniel's prayer brought dramatic results. He had wholeheartedly turned his attention to the Lord to seek Him in prayer and fasting. In that earnest place of prayer, he confessed to God the sin of his people: "*We* have sinned, committed iniquity, acted wickedly and rebelled. . . . Moreover, *we* have not listened to Your servants the prophets" (verses 5–6, emphasis added). Daniel took responsibility for his condition and for that of his nation. Then he cried out for the compassion and presence of the Lord: "O Lord, listen and take action! For Your own sake, O my God, do not delay, because Your city and Your people are called by Your name" (verse 19). We can hear the pathos and grief in his voice as he lifts his prayer to God for his nation.

Having said that repentance is more than an apology to God, we understand that Daniel's prayer is an example of the brokenhearted, passionate cry that literally moves the heart of God and opens the heavens. When there has been emptiness and absence of God's presence, the repentant seeker's heart breaks in response to his need for God. That brokenhearted repentance brings heaven down to us. Basilea Schlink writes:

> What a creative, life-giving power is inherent in repentance! For that reason our Lord Jesus calls the seven churches in Revelation to repent. For the same reason the apostle Peter proclaimed the call to repentance at Pentecost. Repentance is the way to new life. It brings us the Holy Spirit. With repentance the kingdom of heaven is at hand.[8]

Breakthrough to deliverance and freedom is the predictable result of brokenness and repentance for sin before a holy God. It is the pathway to life—God's life being realized in us. True repentance sets us free from sin and death. The apostle Paul taught us: "For the law of the Spirit of life in Christ Jesus has set you free from the law of sin and death" (Romans 8:2). Another translation, *The Living Bible*, gives this powerful rendering: "For the power of the life-giving Spirit—and this power is mine through Christ Jesus—has freed me from the vicious circle [or we could say cycle] of sin and death." What a picture of the human life apart from repentance: a vicious circle of death! Scripture teaches that "the wages of sin is death" (Romans 6:23). And we are caught in this vicious cycle unless we turn to God in repentance.

BREAKING CYCLES

Chuck Pierce, in his teaching on "cycles," describes a *cycle* as a "regularly recurring succession of events or the

period of time occupied by such a succession."⁹ If we find
ourselves in a cycle of life that results continually in the
death of our hopes and dreams, we know that the law of
sin and death is working in us. Cycles of repetitive sin can
be broken by coming to Jesus in repentance and receiving
His power for life. As the Holy Spirit fills us with the life
of God, we will be set free from the control of sin and death.
The Bible also teaches that "where the Spirit of the Lord
is, there is liberty" (2 Corinthians 3:17). We can assume
from this verse that where the Spirit of the Lord is *not*,
there is bondage and captivity. Chuck Pierce teaches that
liberty is "freedom from control, interference, obligation,
and restriction by external or foreign rule."

Every area of bondage in our lives can be exposed and
its power broken as we return to the Lord and receive His
liberty. Jesus promised abundant life for all who believe in
Him (see John 10:10). The Greek word used here for "life"
is *zoe*. When Jesus promised this to us, He promised us a
life full of vitality and prosperous with His purposes.

If past mistakes have caused us to settle for an uneasy
existence filled with guilt and condemnation, we are not
living the life that Christ has promised to give us. So many
times we find ourselves living with a survival mentality—
just trying to get by somehow. We exist under a gray cloud
of yesterday, believing deep down inside that we got what
was coming to us. We need to break through to the new-
ness of life He offers and allow Him to make even our mistakes work for good (see Romans 8:28).

MIRACLES DISPLACE MISTAKES

Abraham lived a life devoted to God, but he did not live
it without making some costly mistakes. As revealed in the

Scriptures, he did not live his life perfectly without sinning against the purposes of God. Regarding the promise of God to give him a son to be his heir, Abraham failed greatly.

Culturally, Sarah was within her bounds to suggest that Abraham allow her maidservant to bear a son for her master since she was barren. This was a common practice in their culture. By listening to the reasoning of his wife, Abraham set aside the promise of God to give him and Sarah a son supernaturally.

Ishmael was the firstborn of Abraham, conceived by Hagar, Sarah's handmaiden. But God was not pleased, because His promise was to give Abraham and Sarah a son—the son of promise. What was not humanly possible, God planned to accomplish supernaturally, allowing Sarah to conceive a son with Abraham in their old age. They did not wait for the supernatural, but tried to make the promise come true in a natural way that they knew would work. The consequences of Abraham's failure to wait for the promise of God are much more far-reaching than his personal grief of family turmoil. All through history, a deadly conflict has caused national suffering to Jewish and Arab peoples.

The New Testament records the grief of Abraham's life when it declares: "He who was born according to the flesh persecuted him who was born according to the Spirit" (Galatians 4:29). Ishmael's mocking of Isaac brought division and strife to Abraham's house (see Genesis 21). God told Abraham to drive out the bondwoman, Hagar, and her son. It was no longer tolerable for the child born of Abraham's compromise (Ishmael) to dwell in the same house with the child born of God's miracle (Isaac). For now, the past was a hindrance to the promise coming to maturity.

The Bible does not elaborate on Abraham's feelings as he sent away his concubine and his son . . . forever. We do have a record of Abraham's anguished prayer that Ishmael might live in the sight of God. And God promised that he would. I am sure that as Abraham handed Hagar and Ishmael their flask of water and loaf of bread, pointing in the direction of the wilderness, and kissing them goodbye, his heart broke.

How many times, like Abraham, have we *compromised* the words God has given us personally? Impatiently, we take matters into our own hands, only to discover that our own plans leave us unfulfilled. One of the results of presumptuous choices that preempt God's plan is grief that will break our hearts.

When God seems to delay His promises to us, as was the case with Abraham, we are challenged to walk in the fear of the Lord and wait upon Him. We will never be able to do naturally what God has spoken He will do supernaturally. Many times the issues and mistakes of the past are the greatest hindrances to breaking through to the miracle of our destinies in God. When the Holy Spirit speaks to our hearts that it is time no longer to tolerate a certain area of compromise that He shows us, we must clean the house of even the fond memories of yesterday. We must quickly obey the voice of the Spirit, and return in our hearts to God and His ways.

BACK TO OUR FIRST LOVE

The prophet Hosea gives us a beautiful, comforting picture of God's loving desire to bring us back to Him when we have chosen another way. God tells Israel through the prophet that, though they have chosen to walk with other "lovers" and have turned from God, He will allure them into the wilderness and speak tenderly to them. We can hear the pathos of this message from God through the prophet as he continues:

> There I will give her [Israel] her vineyard, and make the Valley of Achor or Troubling to be for her a door of hope and expectation. And she shall sing there and respond as in the days of her youth and as at the time when she came up out of the land of Egypt.
>
> HOSEA 2:15 (AMP)

God promises to use Israel's trouble (the wilderness) to bring her back to Himself and give her the joy she had when she was first delivered—rescued from slavery in Egypt. When our hearts break and we walk through our valleys of weeping, God can use even our most grievous mistakes to bring us into a new life of relationship with Him. He can bring us back to our first love as if nothing had ever separated us from Him. How can this be? How can God make anything good out of our terrible mistakes? God promised Israel that He would renew the covenant relationship with them. Then He said:

> I will even betroth you to Me in stability and in faithfulness, and you shall know . . . the Lord. . . . And I will sow her for Myself anew in the land, and I will have pity, mercy and love for her who had not obtained pity, mercy and love, and I will say to those who were not My people, You are My people, and they shall say, You are my God!
>
> HOSEA 2:20, 23 (AMP)

As God cleanses us from our idolatrous and willful mistakes, He will make us faithful and stable to walk in His ways. Then He will "sow us into the land"—make us fruitful to bring others to Him who have not known Him. Not only will we be faithful in our walks with the Lord, but we will also be able to bring others into relationship with Him. That is the power of God to redeem us—to buy back everything we have lost to the enemy.

As we personally break through into a place of overcoming and victory by the redemptive power of the cross, we can have a ministry to reach out to others suffering from similar issues. That which caused us pain and tears can now be a cup of fresh water and encouragement to those who come behind us. We can say, "I made a similar mistake, but God brought me through it to a place of victory. You can follow me as I have followed Christ!" The Scriptures show us that as we are baptized into repentance, as Jesus Himself was baptized, the heavens open:

> John [the Baptist] testified saying, "I have seen the Spirit descending as a dove out of heaven, and He remained upon Him."
>
> JOHN 1:32

We can have this fullness of the Spirit dwelling in us as we yield to a baptism of repentance—not just when we first accept Christ as our Savior. He desires to cleanse us from sin continually. Learning to walk in an attitude of brokenness that results in ongoing repentance and cleansing will bring us to the abundant *zoe*, the life that Jesus promised. We will desire to obey all God's commandments as He reveals Himself to us in His Word.

Our obedience is a vital element to gaining God's favor for personal breakthrough and change. Because of its importance, I want to continue this discussion in the next chapter with a look at the blessings that obedience brings to our lives. Learning to walk in obedience to God's ways is a process that begins with brokenhearted repentance. As we behold God, we will reposition ourselves to align with Him and His ways. In the refreshing presence of Jesus, only one thing will really matter . . . to please Him.

— PRAYER —

Father, I want to be baptized into repentance. Even as John the Baptist baptized for repentance to prepare the way of the Lord, would You immerse me in my own tears of repentance, even now? Break my heart over my sin that I may break through to greater freedom and fulfill my destiny in You. Please open the heavens over me. Amen.

FIVE

INTIMACY WITH GOD

> *Behold, I stand at the door and knock; if any one hears and listens to and heeds My voice and opens the door, I will come in to him and will eat with him, and he [shall eat] with Me.*

REVELATION 3:20 (AMP)

Early one summer morning as I sat quietly on my back porch, sipping my coffee and humming a song, God prepared a lesson for me. So many times He uses ordinary life experiences to teach me more about Himself. This time, He used my unsuspecting neighbor.

My neighbor brought his garbage out to the container behind his house. I thought to myself, *He sure is up early today.* The rest of his household seemed to be still sleeping peacefully. It was then that he realized that he was locked out. He began to knock gently and call his wife's name. This continued for some time. Finally he began pounding on the door and shouting as loud as he possibly could! Frustrated, he sat down outside to wait for someone to wake up and notice that he was not in the house.

The Holy Spirit used this incident to speak to my heart. He revealed to me that many times the Lord stands outside of His own house knocking on the door and calling our names while we sleep. We find ourselves unaware that He has been locked out by our lack of desire to be with Him. That day, I thought of the many times He has knocked on the door of my heart, longing for fellowship with me, and I have been in a state of spiritual slumber and missed the precious moment. I could imagine Him, like my tired neighbor, waiting patiently for me to awaken and invite Him in.

If we will awaken to His voice and open the door, we will experience intimate heart-to-heart talks with Jesus. In that sweet place of communion, He will reveal to us His will and empower us to do it.

I have found that obedience is the natural result and overflow of a loving relationship with God. As we spend time with Him, revelation of His loving sacrifice will break our hearts and woo us to repentance. Repentance then aligns us with His will and causes us to desire to please Him. That God-given desire, placed in our hearts through times of fellowship, results in radical, unrestrained obedience! And obedience will unlock the promise of God and His blessings! Not only will we experience breakthroughs into our personal destinies, but we will enjoy an ever-increasing intimacy with God Himself! It just doesn't get much better than that.

THE BLESSINGS OF OBEDIENCE

It is God's desire to bless His people. He promised Israel that if they would listen to Him and obey Him, they would know great blessing:

If you will listen diligently to the voice of the Lord your God, being watchful to do all His commandments which I command you this day . . . all these blessings shall come upon you and overtake you. . . . The Lord shall open to you His good treasury, the heavens to give the rain of your land in its season, and to bless all the work of your hand; and you shall lend to many nations, but you shall not borrow.

DEUTERONOMY 28:1–2, 12 (AMP)

The promise of the Lord to those who walk in obedience is that blessings will overtake them. Can you imagine looking over your shoulder as you walk in obedience and watching blessings catch up with you? Overtake you? Surprises from the hand of God that we did not earn or work for find their way into our lives through our loving obedience to His word. He promises to rain His blessing upon all that we do (see Deuteronomy 28:12), upon everything that we put our hands to (see Deuteronomy 28:8). Having the blessings of God overtake us is the reward of obedience; it is the joy that comes from living under an open heaven.

In this chapter we will consider four aspects of obedience that follow brokenness and repentance.

OBEDIENCE: LOVE IN ACTION

Few stories define the test of obedience better than the story of Abraham's great sacrifice. After Abraham received the promised blessing of Isaac, his love was tested to see if he would obey regardless of the personal cost to him. God called Abraham His friend, and promised him that he would be a father to many nations. He had been told that his descendants would be more numerous than the dust of

73

the earth or the stars in the sky (see Genesis 13:16; 15:5). After waiting for so many years, Sarah had finally given birth to Isaac. What joy must have flooded the hearts of Abraham and Sarah! The fulfillment of all that had been promised was now possible through this son.

Then we read that God gave Abraham this command: "Take now your son, your only son, whom you love, Isaac, and go to the land of Moriah, and offer him there as a burnt offering on one of the mountains of which I will tell you" (Genesis 22:2). Can you imagine the struggle within Abraham to be obedient to this incredible command? Many years earlier he had left his home and family—all that was familiar—and started on a journey with God in obedience to God's command. After listening to his wife's advice to have a son by her handmaiden, he had obeyed God and cast out Hagar and their son, Ishmael! And now . . . this! How much more could God require? And what of the contradiction this posed to the promises that Abraham had received concerning this heir?

Yet, we read that Abraham rose early in the morning to take Isaac and journey to the mountain of sacrifice. He did not argue or question God's command. And he did not tell Sarah. He would spare her feelings until he saw how the journey turned out.

I do not know if I could be obedient to such a request from God. I do know that at the very least I would have delayed my obedience, hoping that God would change His mind. But Scripture says that Abraham rose early.

Abraham's heart response to God's command was radical, abandoned, trusting. It was a response of a man who understood the principles of a covenant relationship with God. He knew that God, because of His holiness—His very nature—was unable to break His covenant with him that promised an innumerable posterity. In that confidence, Abraham was able to respond to his son's question regarding the sacrifice: "God will provide for Himself the lamb" (Genesis 22:8).

Abraham had told the young servants traveling with them to wait, that he and Isaac would go on up the mount and worship and return to them. As Abraham made the choice of love, he climbed the designated mountain with his son, built the altar, arranged the wood and placed Isaac upon it. But when he lifted the knife to thrust it into his son, heaven opened. The voice of the angel of the Lord stopped Abraham:

> Do not lay your hand on the lad, or do anything to him; for now I know that you fear and revere God, since you have not held back from Me or begrudged giving Me your son, your only son.
>
> GENESIS 22:12 (AMP)

Only then were Abraham's eyes opened to see the provision of a ram caught in the thicket. Abraham named the place, Jehovah-Jireh, which means "the Lord will provide." How many times have we said presumptuously, "God will provide," when we have not obeyed God to go to the designated mountain of worship? It is only in the place where our love is tested that we can expect God's provision. How I long to hear the commendation of God that Abraham received that day: "Now I know that you fear and revere God"! Along with that commendation comes God's miraculous provision.

We must walk in loving and complete obedience to what God has spoken if we are to break through into His provision. What if Abraham had said, "I don't want to make that long journey. One mountain is as good as another. I will go to this or that mount"? I do not believe there would have been a ram on any other mountain. The provision of God was found in the place of complete obedience.

Partial obedience is actually disobedience in the eyes of God. That was apparent in the life of King Saul when God told him to kill the entire enemy he was fighting and to spare nothing of their property. The Scriptures tell us that Saul decided to keep the best for the "noble" purpose of giving it to God. But God considered his actions outright disobedience and Saul lost his position as king over Israel (see 1 Samuel 15:16–23).

Is there something God has told you to do that you may be delaying? Have you tried a shortcut or two hoping still to satisfy the divine mandate? Could it be that the heavens are closed—that the blessings are withheld because of your partial obedience? Could it be that the blessing and provision you have been seeking are on a "different mountain"—waiting for you under an open heaven according to the command of God? If you feel this may be true for you, I encourage you to pray this prayer:

— PRAYER —

Lord, I come to You in humble desire to obey You completely. Please show me anywhere that I have neglected to do what You have spoken to me. I want the heavens to be open over my life. I want the blessings and rewards of obedience to overtake me. I commit myself to taking a position on Your "mountain" of complete obedience, even as I worship You with my whole heart and expect the fulfillment of Your covenant promises. Amen.

OBEDIENCE: THE CHOICE
OF PRAISE

We have seen how God opens the heavens in response to our loving obedience. We can also enjoy the wonderful blessings of God and an open heaven through the obedience of praise. The psalmist declared this wonderful truth regarding praise: "Yet You are holy, . . . You who are enthroned upon the praises of Israel" (Psalm 22:3). It is awesome to think that God is enthroned on our praises and that He will actually dwell with us in the presence of our praises. The King James Version says that God inhabits "the praises of Israel." It is clear from both translations that God wants to dwell in the presence of His praising saints. The word *inhabit* in the Hebrew means literally to "sit down as a judge."[1] In His presence, we will receive the righteous judgment that we desire for our lives and against our enemies—those things that oppose our breakthroughs.

Let your imagination capture for a moment the wonder of God dwelling and establishing His throne in the place of our praises. Tommy Tenney writes that the Japanese character for this word *inhabiting* pictures a great big chair created by our praises for God to sit on.[2] When we praise the Lord, He opens the heavens and sits among us as a righteous judge. The psalmist gives us another dramatic aspect of praise that involves the saints executing justice:

Let the godly ones exult in glory; let them sing for joy on their beds. Let the high praises of God be in their mouth, and a two-edged sword in their hand, to execute vengeance on the nations and punishment on the peoples, to bind their kings with chains and their nobles with fetters of iron, to execute on them the judgment written; this is an honor for all His godly ones. Praise the LORD!

PSALM 149:5–9

To think that our praises become instruments of God to bring judgment on His enemies is almost more than we can comprehend. This understanding of the power of praise is a far cry from singing nice praise songs in a church service in order to feel good. According to the Scriptures, praise becomes a work of God in our lives where He can dwell and execute the purposes of His Kingdom.

Every December, those involved in our ministry gather together to seek the Lord for His direction for the coming year. We ask Him to show us strategies for breaking through to new revelation of His purposes for our personal lives and for the Body of Christ. It seems that many times we do not know what to do with the circumstances of life that seem unchangeable. Sometimes, we simply feel stuck in a rut coping with them.

For the year 2000, the Lord directed us to fast from watching, reading and listening to anything from the media for forty days. In this way, we would be closing our eyes and ears to the world and setting our focus on the Lord. In addition to this fast, we met together for one hour every morning simply to praise the Lord. We invited Him to come and judge the destructive cycles and familiar patterns in our lives as we praised Him. As we implemented the strategy the Lord had given us and enthroned Him on our praises, many people received personal deliverance and breakthroughs. His throne, "His great big chair," had been in our midst. He ruled as Judge against what had been against us!

Do you remember the instruction of the prophet to King Jehoshaphat when he faced his enemies?

"You need not fight in this battle; station yourselves,
stand and see the salvation of the LORD on your behalf."
. . . When [Jehoshaphat] had consulted with the people,
he appointed those who sang to the LORD and those who
praised Him in holy attire. . . . When they began singing
and praising, the LORD set ambushes against the sons of
Ammon, Moab and Mount Seir.

2 CHRONICLES 20:17, 21–22

God told the king that he would not have to fight this
battle. So he wisely appointed the singers to go before the
army and they stood praising the Lord. The result? The
Lord set ambushes against the enemies and they turned on
each other until all three armies were destroyed. All that
the people of Israel had to do was gather the spoil of this
supernatural victory. This Old Testament example teaches
us that the obedience of praise is a powerful connection to
breakthrough and deliverance!

In the New Testament, Paul and Silas discovered the
power of praise in bringing God's justice and vindication.
As they sat in a prison cell, their praises brought forth such
power that "suddenly there came a great earthquake, so
that the foundations of the prison house were shaken; and
immediately all the doors were opened and everyone's
chains were unfastened" (Acts 16:26). The startling words
suddenly and *all the doors* and *everyone's chains* paint for
us the high drama of that supernatural event triggered as
a result of praise. Because of their praises, the heavens were
opened and breakthrough was accomplished—not only for
Paul and Silas, the "praisers," but for everyone! This
remarkable story records that even the jailor (the one holding them captive) and his household were saved.

Perhaps, you need a "suddenly" just as Paul and Silas
did. If you feel as though you are being held captive to some
difficult circumstance—such as physical illness or mental

oppression or relational problems or financial stress—you can follow the apostles' example of releasing praise in your midnight hour. You will experience that same divine power as you begin to sing the praises of God. It is easy to praise when life is kind to us and we are feeling good about things. The test of a praising heart is that we are able to lift our voices to God in praise in our darkest hours. All heaven comes to our aid in those crisis moments to deliver us from an enemy that is too strong for us.

This principle was tested in my own life in the spring of 1994. Our church was experiencing a great outpouring of the Holy Spirit. People were being touched very deeply by the Lord as He swept over us with waves of praise and great joy. Homes were restored, physical illnesses were healed, the emotionally tormented were delivered and backsliders returned!

At the same time, both of my parents were dying. My father had leukemia and I had to make the difficult decision to place him in a nursing home. Because of his weakened condition, he required 24-hour care. On the same day that I took my daddy to the care center, my mother was diagnosed with liver cancer. It was a "midnight hour" for me. It was time for me to make the obedient love choice to praise the Lord in the midst of circumstances that I could not understand and that did not seem fair.

Was the outpouring of the Spirit that had been going on inside the church building going to "work" now inside the nursing home? When I received the news of my mother's report, I walked to the restroom to find a private place to cry. With my head leaning forward on the wall of the restroom, words from a song began to rise from my heart: "Through it all, through it all, I've learned to trust in Jesus, I've learned to trust in God." It was an old song that I had not thought of in years, but it began to flood out of my soul as a fresh new song for that moment. And, then, came the next song: "To God be the glory, to God be the glory, to God be the glory for the things He has done!"

At that moment, the prison door of my despair suddenly swung open and I was free. When I made the choice of obedience, praising Him regardless of how I felt, He rushed to me in a flood of love that is indescribable. I knew that He was going to lead me through that time victoriously. During the next three months, I had several more opportunities to choose to obey Him in praise. Each time His presence and power seemed to increase in my life. By the time their actual deaths came, I was able to release my parents gracefully to the Lord. They died four days apart and as I buried them I could hear the song of praise, "To God be the glory," bubbling out of my heart.

An unlocking happened in my life during that very dark hour that has released me to walk in a greater measure of freedom ever since. Not only did I have a personal victory through the obedience of praise, but I also tapped into my destiny in a new way. My life message became more compassionate and compelling and has led others in similar situations to new levels of relationship with God. As family members and friends—some believers and some unbelievers—watched me walk through loss and death peaceably and freely, some of them found their own prison doors unlocking.

Yes, our personal freedom has a direct result on those around us. One man said to me, "I feel that I am personally changed forever because of watching your relationship with God during these last few days." Unknowingly, I had been praising God, not only in my heart but also with my life! Once I made the choice to obey as I leaned on that restroom wall, the days that followed seemed to flow naturally in the upward direction of praise to God.

Maybe the Holy Spirit is nudging you right now to begin to praise the Lord in the midst of your troubles. I know it does not make sense to the natural mind to begin to sing when you are suffering! However, I can promise you from my personal experience and more importantly from the promise of His Word that obeying Him in praise will result in a powerful demonstration of His love. He simply cannot resist it because He is love. His love will explode upon the scene and you will find yourself lifted out of the prison and positioned in His purposes for your life.

— PRAYER —

Lord, I will praise You and exalt You out of my need for a breakthrough. Like Jehoshaphat, I will go forth to face the enemy under the banner of worship and trust You to set ambushes against the enemy. Even in the prison of my circumstances I will rejoice over Your victory, which is already won. May it result in the deliverance of many! Sit down, my King, as Judge and break the familiar, destructive cycles and patterns of my life as I praise You. Be enthroned upon my worship. Amen.

OBEDIENCE: UNIFIED PRAYER FOR BLESSING

We often think of prayer as something we do before praise, but the Scriptures teach us clearly to *enter* the presence of God with praise and thanksgiving (see Psalm 100). Too often we come to God with a list of petitions and hurriedly ask Him for everything we need, instead of coming to Him as the holy God that He is and bowing in praise and worship before Him. As we learn to cultivate a relationship with God, we will learn God's order of things. We will become more sensitive to the Holy Spirit who can help us to pray for the things we need according to the will of God (see Romans 8:26). Since God has only the best in mind for us, praying according to His will and direction will result in the ultimate blessing of breakthrough!

We are considering the aspects of obedience that are key for us to experience breakthroughs in our personal lives and to be able to walk into our eternal destinies. But we must never lose sight of the fact that as individual believers we will experience complete fulfillment of our divine destiny only in the larger arena of the corporate Body of Christ. This is because His plan has linked us and His individual purposes for our lives together with the lives and purposes of others in the church. Even in the Old Testament, it is clear that the blessing of God dwells in the unity of believers:

> Behold, how good and how pleasant it is for brethren to dwell together in unity! It is like the precious ointment poured on the head, that ran down on the beard, even the beard of Aaron . . . that came down upon the collar and skirts of his garments. . . . [It is] like the dew of . . . Mount Hermon, and the dew that comes on the hills of Zion; for there the Lord has commanded the blessing, even life for evermore.
>
> PSALM 133:1–3 (AMP)

God values the unity of believers as precious; it is to Him like costly fragrant oil covering His Church, saturating us in the anointing. God promises that in that treasured place of unity, He will command the blessing. Before the promised gift of the Holy Spirit fell on the day of Pentecost, the disciples "with one mind were continually devoting themselves to prayer" (Acts 1:14). It was in this atmosphere of corporate prayer in unity of heart and minds that

> . . . suddenly there came from heaven a noise like a violent rushing wind, and it filled the whole house where they were sitting. And there appeared to them tongues as of fire distributing themselves, and they rested on each one of them. And they were all filled with the Holy Spirit and began to speak with other tongues, as the Spirit was giving them utterance.
>
> ACTS 2:2–4

God opened the heavens and sent the promised Holy Spirit to the disciples who were waiting in prayer before Him. After they received the empowerment of the Holy Spirit, those who had previously feared for their lives were full of boldness to preach the Gospel. That very day their personal breakthroughs resulted in the breakthrough of salvation for three thousand souls!

That was not the only occasion when the New Testament Church learned that the power of unity in corporate prayer brought supernatural breakthroughs. Not long after, Peter and John ministered healing to the lame beggar at the gate of the Temple. The religious leaders had them thrown into jail and commanded them not to speak any more in the name of Jesus (see Acts 4:18). After their release, they met with the Church in a corporate prayer meeting. Scripture says they "lifted their voices to God with one accord" (Acts 4:24). God responded instantly to their unified cry, and "the place where they had gathered together was shaken, and they were all filled with the Holy Spirit and began to speak the word of God with boldness" (Acts 4:31). The prayer of united hearts gets God's attention!

After Herod had put James, the disciple, to death, Peter was arrested. On the very night before his scheduled execution, the Church prayed fervently together. God responded with another "suddenly." He sent an angel to the prison cell to awaken Peter and lead him out of his captivity (see Acts 12). If it had not been for the unified prayer of the Church, Peter might have been executed as James had been.

Unified prayer does make a difference in breaking through to our destinies, personal and corporate. Maybe you feel that you do not have a group of people or a whole church to pray in unified fervent prayer for your personal breakthrough. But Jesus promised "if two of you agree on earth about anything they may ask, it shall be done for them by My Father who is in heaven" (Matthew 18:19). As you build godly relationships with others, you can agree with each other in prayer for God to reveal His purposes for your lives. And as you do, you can pray for the church of which you are a part, that God will expand the unity of prayer to others until the church can enjoy the power of corporate prayer and the supernatural results it brings to the Body of Christ.

When I was learning to pray, I enjoyed times with others who had known the Lord and the ways of His Spirit longer than I had. It stirred my personal hunger to develop a prayer life of my own as I observed the powerful results these mature believers experienced. I saw that the Holy Spirit was the One who directed the prayers upon which everyone agreed. I then realized that the power and blessing being received were direct results of being in agreement with the Holy Spirit's desires. In the beginning, I had wondered how it was possible for so many diverse people from a variety of backgrounds to be able to be unified on anything! I discovered their secret: Agree with the Holy Spirit and there will be unity. If there is unity, there is the blessing of answered prayer!

I then began to bring this principle into my personal devotions. I realized that I did not have to have a group of believers around me in order to experience the power of unified corporate prayer. All I had to do was agree with one vitally important Person: the Holy Spirit! The Holy Spirit has been sent to us as the Helper and the Teacher. He will help us and He will teach us how to pray:

> In the same way the Spirit also helps our weakness; for we do not know how to pray as we should, but the Spirit Himself intercedes for us with groanings too deep for words; and He who searches the hearts knows what the mind of the Spirit is, because He intercedes for the saints according to the will of God. And we know that God causes all things to work together for good to those who love God, to those who are called according to His purpose.
>
> ROMANS 8:26–28

As my personal prayer times developed, my relationship with His Spirit increased more and more. And as it turned out, this closer relationship with the Holy Spirit drew me into closer relationship with the Body of Christ. It was then that I began to experience the fullest meaning of the power that is available in the agreement of unified prayer. It seemed as if each time we gathered we had praise reports, which were answers to the previous week's requests. As we obeyed the Lord to pray in unity, He commanded the blessing.

Why don't we agree right now? You and I will pray in agreement, in unity, for your personal breakthrough. Let's believe that as we pray, God will open the heavens and release the necessary power to answer your request.

— PRAYER —

Lord, I agree with my friend for his/her breakthrough. In desperate cries, we turn our focus to You. Only You can change things and bring the release of the answer. Even as Peter was awakened by one of Your "suddenlies" and led out of his captivity into his destiny—would You send a "suddenly" to my friend? You, O Lord, have promised Your blessing on unity. We stand together, unified around Your purposes, and requesting the breakthrough. Release the blessing, precious Redeemer. In Jesus' name we give You this request and thank You for the answer. Amen.

OBEDIENCE: THE PLACE OF INTIMACY

As we choose to live radical lives of obedience, cultivating our relationship with God and with other believers through love, praise and unified prayer, we will be rewarded with intimate communion with the Lord. Jesus promises intimate friendship to all who will receive Him:

Behold, I stand at the door and knock; if any one hears and listens to and heeds My voice and opens the door, I will come in to him and will eat with him, and he [shall eat] with Me.

REVELATION 3:20 (AMP)

Such intimacy is a picture of heart-to-heart fellowship with God. Jesus spoke this invitation after He had shared His messages to the churches with John, the revelator. In essence He was saying to John: "I have given you the necessary information for your sermons to the churches, but if you want it—there's more. My deep desire is to commune with you face to face." We know from reading the Gospels that John was the beloved disciple who had laid his head upon Jesus' breast at the Last Supper. He was the only disciple to remain with Jesus through the agony of the crucifixion. He was the one to whom Jesus had entrusted the care of His mother. But in this latest revelation, Christ says to John, "There's more." Intimacy with the Lord is an ongoing, always unfolding experience. Immediately after he received this invitation for intimate communion with the Lord, John saw "a door standing open in heaven" and received an invitation to "Come up here" (Revelation 4:1).

Even though John was living alone in exile on the island of Patmos because of his faith, his intimate relationship with the Lord resulted in an opening of the heavens to him. He saw Jesus again, this time as Lord and King. John was lifted above the pain and limits of his circumstances to receive greater revelation of God. When we, like John, spend precious times of fellowship with God—dining with Him, talking heart to heart—we can experience a divine breakthrough that will unveil heavenly realities to us. Though our natural situations may seem confining, we, like John, will find as we commune with God that the way out is up. In that place of intimate fellowship, we will gain the heavenly perspective or viewpoint we need for life's situations. Knowing God intimately is the answer to our most perplexing difficulties.

I remember when I was sixteen years old and was looking for my first after-school job. I was frustrated because everyone turned me down with the explanation that they needed someone with experience. I complained to my father, "Daddy, no one will hire me without experience, but how am I supposed to get experience if no one will hire me?" He said with a smile, "Sometimes, honey, it's not what you know but whom you know."

The next day one of the places that had previously turned me down called and offered me a position. "Why did they change their minds?" I wondered.

I learned later that my father had called one of his friends who was a manager in that company. Based on my father's relationship with him, the manager recommended me for the position. Though I did not have the experience for the job, the relationship between my father and the manager opened the door for me. In the same way, I have found that God's heavens are open to me when I stay in intimate relationship with His Son, Jesus. God does not base my access to Him on what I know, but on Jesus, His Son, *whom* I know.

The blood of the Lamb has prevailed for our salvation. The Scriptures declare:

> "And they overcame him [the accuser] because of the blood of the Lamb and because of the word of their testimony, and they did not love their life even when faced with death."
>
> REVELATION 12:11

My relationship to Christ grants me the divine favor of God and access to all that God is. We know that our accuser, Satan, is displaced and thrown down because of the blood of the Lamb. When we are willing to testify of our relationship with Jesus, and to give our very lives for His sake, the heavens are opened to our cries. As we unite with His heart and with other believers in cultivating intimate communion with Christ, we can expect the spiritual atmosphere in our churches to become conducive to the corporate revival our hearts long for.

When Stephen was being stoned for his faith in Christ, he said, "Behold, I see the heavens opened up and the Son of Man standing at the right hand of God" (Acts 7:56). Stephen's intimate relationship with God gave him access to an open heaven when he needed it the most. God received Stephen as a martyr for the Gospel into that open heaven. The result of this and other open heavens was great revival and establishing of churches through the young man Saul (later Paul), who watched Stephen's execution, holding the coats of his murderers.

Ezekiel, an Old Testament prophet who lived during the time of the Babylonian exile, had a dramatic open heaven experience when he was far from home and in a place of captivity. He declared, "While I was by the river Chebar among the exiles, the heavens were opened and I saw visions of God" (Ezekiel 1:1). What a comfort it must have been to him to see visions of God in his captivity! We learn from Ezekiel's experience that regardless of the difficulty of our natural circumstances, intimate relationship with the Lord is possible. Cultivating this intimacy with God is one of the secrets to personal revival, to unlocking our captivity. Whatever our circumstances, they will no longer be able to contain and control us.

Repeatedly, Ezekiel says, "the Spirit lifted me up" (Ezekiel 3:12, 14; 8:3; 11:1, 24; 43:5). If we open the doors of our hearts in obedience to His voice when He knocks, Jesus will come in and commune with us. In turn, He will open the door of heaven to us. When that happens, and we are given divine insight and perspective, breakthrough is at hand! Our intimate relationship with Him has granted us access to the answer we need.

If it is your desire to respond now to Jesus' invitation to enjoy intimate communion with Him, I encourage you to pray this simple prayer.

— PRAYER —

Jesus, it is my desire to know You more. I want to have access to all Your provision and Your purposes through this open door of heaven. I want to learn how to rise above my circumstances and commune with You—to know Your heart. I know that there is more of You for me to discover. Please let me experience personal revival through an intimate relationship with You. Amen.

God longs to respond to the cry of the obedient heart that is willing to seek Him. We understand that the Holy Spirit will show us the areas of our lives that need to change to bring us into loving obedience to the Word of God. As we cultivate a life of intimacy with God, we will desire to repent quickly whenever His light reveals areas that are not pleasing to Him. As we develop lives of praise and prayer, both personal and corporate, we will undoubtedly begin to experience the "suddenlies" of God as He opens the heavens and overtakes us with the blessings He longs for us to have.

SIX

THE BREAKER
ANOINTING

"The breaker goes up before them; they break out, pass through the gate and go out by it. So their king goes on before them, and the LORD at their head."

MICAH 2:13

As I begin this pivotal chapter, I pray that the Holy Spirit will use these pages to reveal this truth to your heart. It was this little verse tucked away in the tiny book of Micah that ignited a new hope and vision in my own heart several years ago. It was this fresh inspiration that motivated me and set me on the course to pursue God's plan for my life wholeheartedly. Previous to this time I had been serving in our church as an assistant pastor to my husband, Dan. From time to time I would preach or I would prophesy. I would stand beside him during altar times and pray for people. Sometimes I would even be invited to speak at a women's meeting in another church or conference. Yet, deep inside of me I knew that there was more that the Lord had called me to do.

When I was a small child, the Lord came to me and called me to preach the Gospel. I was raised in a very conservative denominational church where women were to "keep silent." I can remember telling my parents, "I want to be a preacher when I grow up." Their response was, "Well, honey, you can't be a preacher because you are a girl. Maybe you will marry a preacher and then you can be a preacher's wife."

Still, I would line up my dolls, preach to them and give an altar call. I gave them communion, baptized them in the bathtub and "discipled" them with Bible studies. As I grew up, the dream slipped from my sight and eventually I did what my parents had recommended. I became a preacher's wife. It was great! I enjoyed the ministry with my husband. I was blessed to serve him and our congregation. Yet, I knew something was missing. Once in a while I remembered my childhood visitation, but I dismissed it quickly. I needed the Breaker to break me out of the comfortable identity in which I was living.

I received a brochure in the mail one day that changed my life forever. My friend Cindy Jacobs was leading a conference in Colorado Springs with the theme, "The Voice of God." I decided that I wanted to go and receive from the Lord. I was particularly weary at that time and desired to be in the presence of the Lord and enjoy the dynamic prophetic ministry that I knew would be there.

Cindy was unaware of my depleted condition and asked if I would help with the times of personal ministry to those attending. I felt that would be a blessing to Cindy and would please the Lord if I did so without revealing my personal need and exhaustion. Because of the number of people in attendance, personal ministry the first night took several hours. At the end of the evening, I collapsed into a heap on the floor. The gentleman who came to my aid was Chuck Pierce. He helped me to a chair and then began to declare this Scripture over me:

> "The breaker goes up before them; they break out, pass through the gate and go out by it. So their king goes on before them, and the LORD at their head."
>
> MICAH 2:13

He said, "You have the breaker anointing. You break open your life and pour it out on God's people. Just as the woman with the alabaster box broke open her precious possession and spent it all on Jesus, so do you. Because you are willing to spend and be spent for Him and His purposes, He has placed this special breakthrough anointing upon you today. You will help many people to break out of bondage and direct them through the gates of their destinies. Fear not, for the Lord, the Breaker, will go before you."

From that day until now, that prophetic word has marked my life and ministry. I went to Colorado Springs simply to have a rest and be refreshed, but I experienced the transforming power of God's word for my life. My identity broke forth into the plan and purpose God had for me from the foundations of the world!

It was amazing to watch the Breaker go before me. I never called anyone to ask to minister. I never advertised or promoted my ministry. But suddenly doors began to swing open for me to preach the Gospel. It was as if a news flash had gone out in the spiritual realm! My phone began to ring with requests for me to come and minister.

So, our next key is revealed: *The Breaker is Jesus, the One who has won our breakthrough for us at Calvary. The anointing is the source of power to bring it to pass.*

The verse from the prophet Micah that Chuck Pierce spoke over me says we will first "break out." The way for us, through His power within us, is to break out of our present situations and follow Him into His purposes for our lives. Second, the verse declares that we will "pass through the gate." In ancient times, the gates of a city were considered the place of authority. It was where judgments were rendered in legal matters. So this verse speaks to us of a new authority that will supercede any existing rulership or judgment. When we go behind the Breaker, we are hidden in Him from all accusations and from all judgments that may come against us. Satan has no legal authority to block the way to our destined purpose if we stand behind the provision of the blood of Christ. Our King has gone before us and has established His rule and reign over our lives, having stripped Satan of his authority. Because of His breakthrough, we have the anointing of the Breaker to pass through the gates, which have previously locked us out of His plans for our lives.

> When you were dead in your transgressions and the uncircumcision of your flesh, He made you alive together with Him, having forgiven us all our transgressions, having canceled out the certificate of debt consisting of decrees against us, which was hostile to us; and *He has taken it out of the way,* having nailed it to the cross. When He had disarmed the rulers and authorities, He made a public display of them, having triumphed over them through Him.
>
> COLOSSIANS 2:13–15, EMPHASIS ADDED

Aren't you glad that the Breaker has taken our debt with its hostile obstacles out of the way?

BREAKTHROUGH PROPHESIED

The prophecies of Micah followed the pattern of most prophets who were communicating a message from God to His chosen people. Prophets usually began their proclamations by preaching about the people's disobedience and trying to convince them of their sins, punctuating the sermons with threats of the judgments of God ready to fall. Then followed, in the usual pattern, promises of mercy and deliverance from God. Some prophetic messages addressed the historical situations of that time but also addressed, knowingly or unknowingly, a far-distant future event, often giving assurance of the coming Messiah who would deliver His people from their enemies.

This verse in Micah is one of the most powerful prophecies in the Bible of the coming Messiah. Micah referred to Him as the Breaker—the Anointed One—who would lead the people of Israel to their breakthrough into God's divine promises. The Hebrew word for *Breaker (parats)* means "to break through, to burst out, to break open, or to break in pieces."[1] It implies violence that will burst through any barriers that impede progress. In our desperate situations that have not yielded to our efforts for change, we must look only to the Anointed One, our Breaker, who will lead us on to victory.

Let's look once again at this verse about the Breaker and the verse that precedes it. After Micah declared the judgment that would come because of sin, he declared the Good News of the promise of a coming Deliverer—the Breaker:

"I will surely assemble all of you, Jacob, I will surely gather the remnant of Israel. I will put them together like sheep in the fold; like a flock in the midst of its pasture. . . . The breaker goes up before them; they break

97

out, pass through the gate, and go out by it. So their king
goes on before them, and the LORD at their head."

MICAH 2:12–13

Well-known Bible commentator Matthew Henry clari-
fies for us this wonderful deliverance promised by the coming of the Breaker:

Whereas God had seemed to desert them, and cast them
off, now he will own them, and head them, and help
them through all the difficulties that are in the way of
their return and deliverance (v. 13): *The Breaker has
come up before them,* to break down all opposition, and
clear the road for them; and under his guidance *they have
broken up, and have passed through the gate,* the door
of escape out of their captivity, and have *gone out by it*
with courage and resolution, having Omnipotence for
their van-guard. *Their King shall pass before them,* to
head them in the way, even Jehovah (he is their king) *on
the head of them,* as he was on the head of the armies
of Israel when they followed the pillar of cloud and fire
through the wilderness and when he appeared to Joshua
as *captain of the Lord's host.*[2]

While Micah's message of a coming Breaker had great
import for the time it was written, and was partially fulfilled in the history of Israel, it has even greater import for
us as individuals and for the corporate Body of Christ.
Again, Matthew Henry explains:

This was accomplished when Christ by his gospel gathered together in one *all the children of God that were
scattered abroad,* and united both Jews and Gentiles in
one fold, and under one Shepherd . . . when there were
some added to the church from all parts of the world,
and all men were drawn to Christ by the attractive power

of his cross, which shall be done yet more and more, and perfectly done, when he shall send forth his angels to *gather in his elect from the four winds.* . . . Christ is the church's King. . . . He is the *breaker, that* . . . broke through them, that rent the veil, and opened the kingdom of heaven to all believers.[3]

Let us see how we might appropriate the wonderful power of this Breaker who "goes up before" as we seek God for breakthroughs to personal destiny and corporate revival.

One note before we begin. It is imperative that we not ignore the prophetic proclamation of the sins of our day. We must repent of and renounce all sin, and choose to follow the Breaker so that we can walk in the gracious promises of redemption that He bought for us at Calvary. It is because of Calvary that we are able to appropriate the life and power of Christ.

THE AUTHOR AND FINISHER

In chapter 1 we discovered the urgent need that we have to get to Jesus in order to experience personal breakthrough from the destructive power of the past and the present hindrances blocking us. "Getting to Jesus" means getting to know Him as a Person we can relate to. In addition, He is our model for living. If we can find out how He did it, then we will have an example to follow as we travel on the road to complete fulfillment.

Jesus is the "author and finisher of our faith" (Hebrews 12:2, KJV). He is the One who has written the book of your life. Isn't it amazing to realize that all you have to do is submit the blank pages to Him? He promises to write His will and plan upon the pages of your heart. Then He promises to give you the faith and power to complete those plans. What He has started in you, He will complete. In fact, from His perspective, it is already done! Not only has Jesus walked into your past and cleansed you of its every effect by His blood, but also He has already walked into your future and established your victory. He stands at the finish line of the race and declares that you are the winner of the prize.

How is this possible? Because He is not limited to the now; He frees up all things including time. As the Finisher of your faith, He declared "It is finished" two thousand years ago (see John 19:30). He looked through the ages and found you in the Father's heart. His faith stood for you and God's purposes for your life *then,* and His faith works *now* to bring you through to complete victory.

It is He, the Breaker, who has gone before us; even the gates of hell will not prevail against us! Hell's railing judgments and accusations will not be able to stop us if we go behind Him. Because He overcame the obstacles of death and the grave, He has given us access to the same overcoming power. So let us "consider Him who has endured such hostility by sinners against Himself, so that you may not grow weary and lose heart" (Hebrews 12:3). Let's consider the Breaker's life. He broke through every obstacle that opposed His purpose and won the ultimate victory. What was His secret? What was His source of such incredible power?

THE SOURCE OF HIS POWER

Christ, as the Son of God, was fully God. But as the Son of man, He was also fully man. So the source of His power to live as a man without sin and to perform all of the will of the Father cannot be attributed to His deity but rather to His dependence on the power of the Holy Spirit, as He Himself declared:

> "The Spirit of the Lord is upon Me, because He anointed Me to preach the gospel to the poor. He has sent Me to proclaim release to the captives, and recovery of sight to the blind, to set free those who are oppressed, to proclaim the favorable year of the Lord."

LUKE 4:18–19

We also must learn dependence on that anointing of the Holy Spirit to enable us to walk without sin and fulfill our divine destinies in God. In complete obedience, Jesus humbled Himself, emptying Himself of all the privileges of His deity. He became like us in every way, except without sin. The apostle Paul says that although Jesus existed in the form of God, He

> did not regard equality with God a thing to be grasped, but emptied Himself, taking the form of a bond-servant, and being made in the likeness of men. Being found in appearance as a man, He humbled Himself by becoming obedient to the point of death, even death on a cross.

PHILIPPIANS 2:6–8

Humility prefaces all we receive from God, beginning with salvation. In order to be filled with and empowered by the Holy Spirit we must humble ourselves before God and seek Him. Just as we must acknowledge our need of God in order to receive eternal life, so we must humble ourselves and admit our dependence on Him in order to be empowered to receive our personal breakthroughs.

Jesus acknowledged His complete dependence on the Father when He declared to His disciples:

> I am able to do nothing from Myself—independently, of
> My own accord; but as I am taught by God and as I get
> His orders. . . . I do not seek or consult My own will—I
> have no desire to do what is pleasing to Myself, My own
> aim, My own purpose—but only the will and pleasure
> of the Father Who sent Me.

> JOHN 5:30 (AMP)

How did Jesus walk in perfect obedience to the will of the
Father? By humbling Himself to receive the anointing of
the Holy Spirit.

The Holy Spirit did not just anoint Jesus to heal diseases
and perform miracles; He also empowered Him for the radical obedience that He needed in the face of unthinkable
suffering. The Scriptures tell us that Jesus was perfected
and learned obedience through the things He suffered (see
Hebrews 2:10; 5:8). Jesus was not coming from a place of
disobedience, as we are, yet in a way we do not fully understand, He had to learn obedience through suffering. What
we do understand is that this anointing that was upon
Jesus—our Breaker—broke the power of sin and death that
was destroying the human race. Scripture explains:

> For as through the one man's disobedience [Adam] the
> many were made sinners, even so through the obedience
> of the One [Jesus] the many will be made righteous.

> ROMANS 5:19

The result of humility is always the exaltation of God.
The Scriptures tell us that because of the radical obedience
of Christ to the will of the Father, humbling Himself to
suffer death on the cross,

> God highly exalted Him, and bestowed on Him the
> name which is above every name, so that at the name

of Jesus every knee will bow, of those who are in heaven and on earth and under the earth, and that every tongue will confess that Jesus Christ is Lord, to the glory of God the Father.

PHILIPPIANS 2:9–11, EMPHASIS ADDED

Sometimes we feel that we cannot endure the painful situations we have to suffer, whether physically, emotionally, spiritually or relationally. Although Jesus came to alleviate suffering, as we have seen, He also said to His followers that in the world they would have tribulation (see John 16:33). The Gospel does not promise to keep us from all trouble, but it does promise to give us power to endure and to overcome the world as Jesus did. At times, as we lay down our personal comfort and choose the path of obedience to God, we will suffer. But it is that path, as difficult as it may seem, that will lead us to fulfilling our life's purpose.

It was from a position of personal pain and disappointment that Paul wrote these words:

For momentary, light affliction is producing for us an eternal weight of glory far beyond all comparison, while we look not at the things which are seen, but at the things which are not seen; for the things which are seen are temporal, but the things which are not seen are eternal.

2 CORINTHIANS 4:17–18

Paul's leadership and authority had been opposed by a certain group of people who had created crisis in the church at Corinth. Paul had made a visit to try to correct the problem but was unable to accomplish his objective. Instead he endured open hostility to his message (see 2 Corinthians 2:5–8; 7:12) and sorrowfully returned to Ephesus. Later, he received good news: Events had turned in Corinth and the opposition had been greatly diminished (see 2 Corinthians 7:6–16).

Many times we, like Paul, will suffer even in our obedience. Yet we can be assured that an "eternal weight of glory" is being produced in our lives that will outshine the worst of conditions. It is the power of His presence in our lives that gains for us our eventual breakthrough! I believe this is why Paul encourages us not to "lose heart" (2 Corinthians 4:1, 16).

CONSIDER HIM!

In order to relate our suffering to a larger divine perspective, let's consider Him in His suffering.

Think of the pain Jesus suffered from being misunderstood and rejected by His own family and friends. There were times when they literally thought He had lost His senses (see Mark 3:21). And rejection was not limited to His home— it happened at church! The mocking and challenging of the Pharisees, the religious leaders of His day, must have cut Him deeply as they spewed out their hatred for Him. They slandered His character, considering Him to be a hoax at best, a demoniac at worst. He lived with the constant stigma of their disapproval and envy, which eventually turned to hatred. Even His disciples who loved Him and walked with Him for three years failed to understand Him. Often He chided them for their unbelief and lack of faith. Consider also how Jesus suffered when His cousin John the Baptist was beheaded (see Matthew 14:10). And we can read how He wept over the holy city, Jerusalem, because she had missed her day of visitation (see Matthew 23:37).

Dare we continue—to think of the suffering and agony in the Garden of Gethsemane? There alone, as His friends slept, Jesus bore our sorrows and wrestled with His own humanity, asking the Father if there were another possible way to bring redemption other than drinking this cup (see Mark 14:36). Imagine also the betrayal of his friend Judas—one who had walked daily with Him for three years and then sold Him for thirty pieces of silver. What pain accompanied that deadly kiss Judas gave Him as a sign to His captors (see Mark 14:44–45)? Do you remember how His friend Peter disowned and denied Him three times (see Mark 14:66–72)? Surely those were moments when Jesus needed him most.

We cannot leave this brief glimpse of Jesus' obedience in the midst of terrible suffering without gazing for a moment at Calvary. Only the Holy Spirit can paint that picture of His suffering in your mind. Do you see the love in His eyes? Do you see the flow of blood coming from His pierced side? Can you hear the insults of the soldiers and even of the thieves crucified beside him? Do you see His arms stretched out in reckless abandon to the will of His Father? Can you sense the agony of His aloneness as He cries out, "My God, My God, why have You forsaken Me?" (Mark 15:34)?

The ultimate sacrifice of Jesus on the cross released the greatest power from God for salvation that the world will ever know. Christ's inestimable suffering to complete His perfect obedience to the Father has given us the right to become children of God by believing in Him (see John 1:12). I have found that if I take a few moments daily to gaze upon the suffering of Jesus' last days on earth and especially upon the cross, I gain courage to press past my own sufferings for the goal of "the upward call"—a life fulfilled in knowing Him (see Philippians 3:10–14).

Probably, some of the greatest suffering I have endured has involved the loss of some precious relationships. Because of misunderstandings, disappointments and divisions, I have had people I loved dearly walk out of my life without even a word of farewell. Of course, this is a common situation in most churches some time or another. It is certainly one of the "occupational hazards" of pastoring. I could never protect myself from getting emotionally involved in people's lives. If they rejoiced, then so did I. If they wept, then so did I. They had my heart completely. So, when they exited from my life, they took a piece of my heart with them. It felt as though my heart was being ripped from my chest each time.

Yet, as I would gaze upon Jesus and see how He endured the misunderstanding, betrayal and abandonment of those He loved, I would receive comfort and courage to continue pursuing His purposes for my life. In that place of considering Him, the precious presence of the Holy Spirit would bring me out of the place of death and infuse me with the power of resurrection—the power to arise and shine (see Isaiah 60:1)! Yes, He empowered me to love again. Instead of putting up walls of self-protection and preservation, I was able to open my heart again to those He entrusted to me. In some of those previous relationships, the Lord has brought restoration and reconciliation. In others, I am still waiting. Yet, I know my future and fulfilled purposes are not locked up in my past because the Breaker has gone before me!

With this understanding, we can take heart. Our obedience to the will of God may involve suffering, but it will release His power in our lives for personal breakthrough to such victory that we never believed possible.

THE CLASSROOMS OF JESUS

I have wondered what Jesus' classrooms were like in which He learned to endure suffering in order to see the power of God released—power to heal the sick, raise the dead and cast out demons. I think of two in particular: the classrooms of temptation and prayer. When Christ embraced the sufferings of His humanity, it seems as though they were transformed into the stuff of which power is made; that through His humble obedience to the will of the Father, anointing for the miraculous was released.

The classroom of Jesus' temptation in the wilderness was extremely significant. Scripture teaches that after Jesus' baptism by John, the Holy Spirit led Him into the wilderness to be tempted by the devil. Jesus persisted there for forty days in fasting and prayer. Throughout the temptation that He suffered in that place, Jesus established His divine authority over the devil. He did not base it upon Himself or His efforts, but solely upon the written Word of God. To every challenge of the devil He declared, "It is written" (see Luke 4:1–13).

Jesus came out of that place of temptation "in the power of the Spirit" (verse 14). It was then that He announced publicly to the people in the synagogue the source of His power: "The Spirit of the Lord is upon Me, because He has anointed Me" (verse 18). Power was released from that place of temptation that He suffered, power to begin His public ministry of healing and miracles and declaring the Good News.

The place of prayer in Jesus' life is another significant classroom. Throughout His ministry, Jesus went aside to pray and fellowship with the Father, at times spending entire nights in prayer (see Luke 6:12). He knew that the source of His power was not only the written Word of God, but also the place of communion with His Father. As He communed with His Father, He humbled Himself in the weakness of His humanity and learned to release the divine power and anointing of the Holy Spirit.

Not only did His classroom of prayer bring Him into sweet fellowship with His Father, but it also strengthened Him. In His final hours, as He suffered and wrestled in the agony of His humanity in the Garden of Gethsemane, He arose from that place of prayer in the power of the Holy Spirit to face boldly those who came to arrest Him. He even performed a miracle in that place, restoring the cut-off ear of one of the soldiers (see Luke 22:51).

Until the very end, His most radical point of obedience, Jesus was in His own personal classroom of prayer, learning the way of extravagant love and submission to the will of the Father. Laying down His life utterly, He breathed His last breath and committed His spirit into the hands of the Father. In that instant, even nature responded to that ultimate act of suffering and obedience. The earth shook, rocks were split, tombs were opened and many bodies of the saints who had fallen asleep were raised to life again (see Matthew 27:51–52). Supernaturally, the veil in the Temple was torn in two from top to bottom.

Our wonderful Breaker, Jesus, broke the power of the enemy that day to complete our redemption. That ultimate obedience made it possible for the power of resurrection life to be released and to fill His tomb three days later as the Father and the Holy Spirit reclaimed Him from the dead. As we choose to follow Christ, our Breaker, we will attend the classrooms of temptation and prayer and we will be able to experience this resurrection power in our lives as well.

THE SOURCE OF OUR POWER

Thus we see that through the anointing of the Holy Spirit, Jesus was obedient to His Father. This anointing was the source of victory for His life, death and resurrection. Jesus, Himself, did not rely on His own strength or even the privilege of His deity to fulfill His divine destiny.

The source of our power to fulfill our divine destinies is outside of us, as well. It is not natural but supernatural. We too must learn to rely completely on the power of the Holy Spirit working in us as Jesus did. We must be humbly dependent on Him: "We have this treasure in earthen vessels, so that the surpassing greatness of the power will be of God and not from ourselves" (2 Corinthians 4:7).

You may be reading this book because you are discouraged by the weakness of your humanity that so often runs out of strength and ingenuity in trying to break through to your purpose. Your own abilities, resolve, education and even consecration have not been enough to break you out of the ordinary and break you through to the extraordinary plans of God for your life. That is actually a good place to be, because we will never experience true change through efforts of our human strength.

The apostle Paul declared that whatever he counted as gain before, he now considered rubbish in order to "gain Christ" (Philippians 3:8). We, like the apostle Paul, must consider our "gains"—educational credentials and qualifications, intellect and talents, plans and programs—as "rubbish" in order to gain Christ. Paul also said that he put "no confidence in the flesh" (Philippians 3:3). Instead, he would glory only in the cross of Christ. We must follow his example here as well if we are to release the true source of power dwelling in us—the Anointed One, the Breaker—who alone can guarantee our breakthroughs.

By choosing to die to our own carnal desires, dreams and determinations, and choosing to live in humble obedience to His will regardless of the cost, we identify with the death of Christ. Jesus said, "If anyone wishes to come after Me, he must deny himself, and take up his cross and follow Me" (Matthew 16:24). If we are going to follow the Breaker through the gates of breakthrough, we must do it His way. Dr. Fuchsia Pickett says it like this: "To the degree that you are willing to give up your will, your way, your words, your walk, your worship and your warfare—to that degree will you find the will of God for your life."

Through this exchange of the self-life for His life, we position ourselves to experience His resurrection power as well. The apostle Paul exhorted us to have the same attitude that was in Christ, who emptied Himself of His privileges and humbled Himself, being obedient to the point of death (see Philippians 2:5–8). The result of His sacrificial obedience was His victorious resurrection and exaltation to His Father's right hand. That wonderful resurrection power to live a victorious life awaits us as we choose to be dependent on the power of the Holy Spirit.

Instead of living lives of defeat as victims of our circumstances, we will be victorious overcomers by the power of His life in us! In fact, the Scriptures promise that "we overwhelmingly conquer through Him who loved us" (Romans 8:37). As we die to ourselves, our lives will then be "hidden with Christ in God" (Colossians 3:3). The power of the blood of the cross will cover our past sinful identities so that we reflect the life of Christ as His Spirit becomes our Source of strength and power. We can then say with Paul: "It is no longer I who live, but Christ lives in me" (Galatians 2:20). As we learn not to put confidence in our flesh but to glory in Christ alone, we will join with Paul in saying, "I can do all things through Him who strengthens me" (Philippians 4:13).

Many times when we grow impatient for a breakthrough in a painful situation or relationship, we are tempted to take matters into our own hands and rush ahead of God's provision and power. The prophet Isaiah discovered the way to find new strength as we position ourselves in God's presence and wait for His strategy. He declared:

> He gives strength to the weary, and to him who lacks might He increases power. . . . Those who wait for the LORD will gain new strength; they will mount up with wings like eagles, they will run and not get tired, they will walk and not become weary.
>
> ISAIAH 40:29, 31

If we choose to wait on the Lord, He will cause us to mount up above our situations like the eagle that soars around the mountain peaks. From that exalted perspective, we will understand the perspective of heaven and be given the power and strength to accomplish all that God ordains for us.

Someone once told me that the "cutting edge" I desired for my life and ministry would be found in the place where I came to the end of myself. That statement has become a reality for me as I have discovered that my strength is insufficient to break through the obstacles to my personal destiny in God.

On one occasion, though filled with good intentions, I was striving in my own strength to bring the Word of the Lord to pass in my life. I devoted hours to meaningless effort. Frustrated by my lack of results, I finally decided to pray. As I prayed, the Holy Spirit directed me to Job 38. I read there the questions that God asked Job, and those questions pierced my own heart:

> "Where were you when I laid the foundation of the earth? . . . Have you ever in your life commanded the morning and caused the dawn to know its place[?] . . . Have you entered into the springs of the sea or walked

in the recesses of the deep? . . . Do you know the ordinances of the heavens, or fix their rule over the earth? Can you lift up your voice to the clouds, so that an abundance of water will cover you? Can you send forth lightnings that they may go and say to you, 'Here we are'?"

VERSES 4, 12, 16, 33–35

In the light of those questions, I understood my finiteness in a new way. I realized then that my only hope for victorious breakthrough was to yield to the conquering Christ in me, "the hope of glory" (Colossians 1:27). My only hope for victory in that impossible situation lay in the fact that the same Spirit that raised Christ from the dead dwells in me (see Romans 8:11).

The resurrection power of God that came into that tomb on the third day and raised Christ out of death dwells in us if we are born again. If we are yielding to the Spirit of God and depending on His power, we can say with the apostle Paul, "In Him we live and move and exist" (Acts 17:28). As we choose to cultivate that intimate relationship with Christ, and determine to put no confidence in our flesh, we are positioning ourselves for the breakthrough that His resurrection power will work in and through our lives. In Him the natural human limits are broken and the impossible is attainable. The boundaries or "boxes" of our past experiences and identities are destroyed and the possibilities for breakthrough are endless.

Are you weary? At your wits' end? Do you, like me, realize that you do not have the power you need to be victorious? As we wait in the presence of God, the divine power of the Breaker will grow within us. At the strategic appointed time, the Breaker anointing will break out and pass through every opposing gate to our purposes. Our part is to follow behind Him in humble, dependent obedience. His power will do the rest!

— PRAYER —

Precious Lord, I want to know You as the Breaker and I desire to receive the Breaker anointing in my life. Today, I make a commitment to embrace the cross, deny myself and follow You. I need Your power to break out of where I am and to break through the obstacles that stand in the way of Your purposes for my life. Thank You for going before me. I'm right behind You! Amen.

SEVEN

PREPARE FOR POWER

Have you ever wished that you had more power in your life and ministry? In my early Christian walk I would look longingly at some of the great Christian leaders and see the signs of God's power demonstrated in their lives and ministries. I would think, *I want what they've got. Whatever it is—I want it!* One day the Holy Spirit asked me very sweetly, *Why? Why do you want that anointing?* At that moment, He shone the light of His truth into my heart and revealed to me my impure motive for wanting God's power in my life.

It was not easy to face that revelation. I saw that I wanted God's supernatural power to flow through my life so that I would have position and personal recognition, rather than desiring for God's Kingdom to be established and *His* fame to be made known. My heart broke over my deplorable condition. As I repented and cried out for God's mercy, the Holy Spirit changed my heart. In the years that have followed, through many trials, God has taught me that manifesting His supernatural power is the natural overflow of a life lived in His presence.

When faced with impossible situations, I discovered the next key to change: *If breakthrough is not dependent upon personal ability and strength, but upon the power of the Holy Spirit, then our job is to prepare for Him.*

Do you remember the angel's answer to the virgin Mary when she asked how it could be possible physically for her to bear a son? The angel answered: "The Holy Spirit will come upon you, and the power of the Most High will over-shadow you" (Luke 1:35). The angel quieted her fears by changing her focus from herself to the supernatural power of the Holy Spirit. In essence he said to her, "Mary, it's not about you; it's about the presence and power of the Holy Spirit who will work in you. Just step into the shadow of the Most High. He'll do the rest!"

My First Miracle

The first time miraculous power was manifested in my ministry, it actually shocked me. A young girl who had scoliosis (curvature of the spine) came to the altar for heal-ing. Her mother said she was scheduled for surgery that week. I placed my hand upon her spine and prayed a sim-ple prayer. Then, I felt her spine literally pop and straighten under my hand.

Later that night as I lay in bed, I wept. My tears of grat-itude to God for touching and healing that young girl were mixed with confusion and pain in my own heart. I could not understand why the power of God would flow through me to bring healing to her when I am suffering from the same disease and am not healed.

I felt hypocritical because I could not receive my own healing. That night the Lord taught me an important les-son. He answered my anguish in quiet tones: *I want you to know and always remember that it is not about you; it is about Me and My presence.* I learned that it is simply my responsibility to prepare the way for Him. If through my repentance, my worship or my message, a place is prepared for His power and presence to work, then I have pleased Him and He will come to that place!

CONSECRATION: PREPARATION FOR VISITATION

In chapter 2 we mentioned David's first attempt to bring the Ark of the Covenant back to Jerusalem by ox cart. Uzzah reached out to steady the Ark when the oxen stumbled, but he had not prepared himself for the power that he experienced when he touched the Presence. The power of God broke out against him and he died on the spot. The literal rendering of David's words about that event is: *The Lord had broken through a breakthrough* (see 1 Chronicles 13:11).

Uzza broke through to God's presence but he did it without the *preparation of consecration.* It is as if he made an opening or breach between the temporal and the eternal. Through that opening, came the unlimited, unrestrained power of God. Human flesh cannot casually reach into the eternal Glory and remain untouched.

David discovered that consecration is a necessary part of preparation to receive a visitation of God's presence and power. Before the next attempt to move the Ark, David told the Levites:

> *"Consecrate* yourselves both you and your relatives, that you may bring up the ark of the Lord God of Israel to the place that I have *prepared* for it. Because you did not carry

117

it at the first, the LORD our God made an outburst on us, for we did not seek Him according to the ordinance."

1 CHRONICLES 15:12–13, EMPHASIS ADDED

David learned this principle—consecration as part of the preparation for coming into the presence of God—from biblical precedents (see 1 Chronicles 15:15). Moses was instructed by God to prepare the people for a visitation:

"Go to the people and consecrate them today and tomorrow, and let them wash their garments; and let them *be ready* [prepared] for the third day, for on the third day the LORD will come down on Mount Sinai in the sight of all the people."

EXODUS 19:10–11, EMPHASIS ADDED

Joshua followed the example of Moses as he was preparing the people of Israel to cross the Jordan and possess their inheritance. Joshua 3:5 says: "Consecrate yourselves, for tomorrow the LORD will do wonders among you." In both of these examples, when God's people prepared themselves to be in His presence, power followed. In Moses' day, the mountain quaked and there was thunder and lightning. Joshua experienced the powerful demonstration of God as the waters of the Jordan rolled back before the Ark of the Presence and the consecrated people crossed over into the land of promise (see Joshua 3:14–17).

Biblical teaching on this subject is not limited to the Old Testament, of course. John the Baptist's was the voice in the wilderness crying, "Make ready the way of the LORD" (Luke 3:4). John's message was one of repentance to prepare the hearts of the people for the visitation of their Messiah. After receiving John's baptism, Jesus was led by the Spirit into the wilderness to be tested by the devil. When

He completed that time, He came out in "the power of the Spirit" (Luke 4:14).

It seems to me that the Lord still brings His people to the wilderness to prepare them for His purposes and power in their lives. The wilderness is a place that is usually outside of our familiar comfort zones. It is a place of solitude and a place of testing. It is also a place of preparation and consecration. It is in the wilderness that we find ourselves gaining clarity, focus and direction as we humble ourselves before the Lord. In this place of aloneness our hearts are tested and tried and we are brought to a crossroads. Here, we decide if we will be completely God's and go the distance—no matter what happens. When we choose to set our lives apart for Him and His desires, this is consecration. In speaking prophetically to Israel, Hosea declared these words of the Lord:

> "Therefore, behold, I will allure her, bring her into the *wilderness* and speak kindly [upon her heart[1]] to her. Then I will give her her vineyards from there, and the valley of Achor [the place of trouble[2]] as a door of hope. And she will sing there as in the days of her youth, as in the day when she came up from the land of Egypt."
>
> HOSEA 2:14–15

As God's people today, we can apply the principles of this prophecy to our lives. In modern language the Lord could be saying to us: "I am going to draw you aside, outside of your comfort zone and to a place of aloneness with Me. In this place, I will talk heart to heart with you. I will place My desires within you. I will grant to you, in that place, fruitfulness. The place of your past troubles will be behind you and a door of hope will open to you as you gain My perspective. As your heart fills with hope, you will find that once again you have a song in your heart. You will feel the freedom you first felt when I delivered you from your past bondages and gave you a new life."

Even as God placed John the Baptist in the wilderness as a "voice" of preparation for His people, His voice today is still speaking to us through His Word and by His Spirit in our wilderness places. "The voice of the LORD shakes the wilderness; the LORD shakes the wilderness of Kadesh," the psalmist says (Psalm 29:8). One of the Hebrew meanings for *shakes*[3] is "to give birth." Therefore, the voice of the Lord brings to birth. *Kadesh*[4] is the same Hebrew word used for *consecrate,* such as when God told Moses to *consecrate* the people and prepare them for His visitation.

So we can say that God's voice will bring to birth His purposes in the place of consecration. When we consecrate ourselves—set ourselves apart unto God—we are positioned for the powerful birthing of His purposes in our lives. We, in our wildernesses, are preparing the way of the Lord as we embrace the message of repentance and allow it to work in us a lifestyle of consecration and holiness.

VISITATION AND HABITATION

When we prepare for the Lord to come to us, we are getting ready for the miraculous. To gain our breakthroughs we need the power of the Breaker, Himself. What if the Breaker came to your house? To your church? To your ministry? The long agonizing times of trial and error would be over. The frustrations of expending strength and energy in futile attempts to change things would be gone. What if revival power knocked at your door and broke through for you? It is possible, but we must be ready. We must make a place for Him to reside. If we want His power, we must prepare for His presence.

Second Kings 4 gives us a prophetic picture of this concept. Here we read that a prominent Shunammite woman perceived that Elisha was a man of God. Whenever he passed through her town, he received her hospitality by stopping in for a meal. There came a day that she was no longer satisfied with those short visits. She persuaded her husband to build a little room and furnished it for the prophet's needs. He no longer just stopped by for a meal; he *lived* there whenever he was in town.

I wonder if you have come to a similar place in your relationship with the Lord. Is the occasional visit with God no longer enough for you?

I remember when I came to that place. I no longer was satisfied to answer an altar call, have someone pray for me and feel a "touch" from God. I wanted God to be with me in a very tangible way on a daily basis. I had only known Him by the occasional Sunday visits I had with Him at church. I wanted that same sense of His presence with me all the time. And so, I began to prepare a place for Him by consecrating my life to Him every day—not just on Sundays for a church service. I discovered that just as the prophet enjoyed the upper chamber and rested there, so God enjoys the place of prominence I have made for Him.

As we make provision for His presence by being hospitable to Him and to His preferences, He comes to rest. The psalmist said, "Surely I will not enter my house, nor lie on my bed; I will not give sleep to my eyes or slumber to my eyelids, until I find a place for the LORD, a dwelling place for the Mighty One of Jacob" (Psalm 132:3–5). David declared that he would make God's comfort a priority over his own. He began to describe the place of God's habitation when he said, "Let us go into His dwelling place; let us *worship* at His footstool. Arise, O LORD, to Your *resting place*, You and the ark of Your *strength*" (verses 7–8, emphasis added). Worship is a place where God feels at home. It is a place of His strength and power. As our lives become worship to Him and we present ourselves to Him as *"a living and holy sacrifice"* (Romans 12:1, emphasis added), then we have built a place of resting for Him. A release of His power will come forth.

RESURRECTION POWER

The woman who had anticipated the prophet Elisha's needs and made provision for him was surprised with an unexpected and unasked for blessing. Though she was barren, she conceived and bore a son (see 2 Kings 4:16–17). When God comes among us, He often blesses us beyond what we could imagine! Just as He surprises us with more than we could dream, He also tests our hearts with that blessing.

This happened to the woman when her miracle child became sick and died. She reacted without hesitation. She did not curse the prophet or question God. Instead, she took the body of her dead son and placed him on the prophet's bed. She then saddled her donkey, told her husband that all was well and pursued Elisha. She knew where the power was and she already had a place prepared for the miracle she needed.

Elisha saw the woman coming to him from a distance and prepared to meet her. He said to his servant, "Behold, there is the Shunammite. Please run now to meet her and say to her, 'Is it well with you? Is it well with your husband? Is it well with the child?'" (2 Kings 4:25–26). What a beautiful picture this is of the Lord! When we come to Him with our desperate, impossible situations, He rises to meet us.

After hearing what had happened, Elisha followed her home. When Elisha arrived, he prayed to the Lord and stretched himself over the dead child. He did this two times and the child's life returned to him. He then presented the child back to his mother (see 2 Kings 4:27–36).

This is a wonderful picture of breakthrough and of revival. As we prepare our hearts and lives, homes and churches for His presence through repentance, consecration and worship, a place of habitation is being built for God. In that place, the miraculous will occur. Whatever is impossible will be overshadowed by the power of the Holy Spirit. Some unexpected, awesome things that go beyond our dreams will surprise us! Some things that we thought were dead forever will begin to breathe again.

Actually that is what *revival* means—to be revived or resuscitated. God will stretch Himself over us and even over our dead dreams and visions and release His power. His power is resurrection power! He will fill us with this power and we in turn can also minister with signs and wonders that will revive others (see Mark 16:17–18). Paul wrote that "if the Spirit of Him who raised Jesus from the dead dwells in you, He who raised Christ Jesus from the dead will also give life to your mortal bodies through His Spirit who dwells in you" (Romans 8:11).

Imagine! Resurrection power is inside of you! The Breaker has placed His anointing for breakthrough and revival within you! Maybe you just have never realized *Who* is with you.

BLINDERS TO THE BREAKTHROUGH OF POWER

When disillusioned disciples were walking on the road to Emmaus after the death of Jesus, they said (to the unrecognized resurrected Christ), "We were hoping that it was

He who was going to redeem Israel. Indeed, besides all this, it is the third day since these things happened" (Luke 24:21). They did not realize that their Hope was walking with them. Their eyes were prevented from recognizing Him.

I wonder if it was the disappointment that blinded them. When Jesus began to open their eyes to the Scriptures, their hearts began to burn within them. As they approached their destination, "they urged Him, saying, 'Stay with us, for it is getting toward evening, and the day is now nearly over'" (Luke 24:29).

I believe that Jesus still wants to hear His disciples invite Him to *stay* and to reside with them today. Even if we are disappointed and do not understand some things, He desires to open the eyes of our understanding (see Ephesians 1:18) so that His resurrection power can be seen and then released to us and through us. As He broke bread with them that evening, their eyes were opened.

When the Almighty God hears our hungry repentant cries and our abandoned worship, and sees our consecrated lives, He moves in. He feels right at home and breaks bread with us. The place of His residing Presence is a place where His resurrection power will be revealed. Just as the disciples did not realize who was in their midst, maybe we do not realize that our breakthrough is closer than we imagine!

Fear is another blinder. Following the death of Jesus, the disciples were hidden behind locked doors because of their fear of the Jews. They were frightened that the religious leaders would target them next (see John 20:19). Even though Mary Magdalene had brought them a report of the resurrection of the Lord, they refused to believe her (see Mark 16:11). Unlimited power had been released but their fear prevented them from believing it.

Sometimes when we are disappointed or afraid, something inside of us shuts and locks. It is the door of our hearts.

We withdraw into our problems and bolt the door. The power that is available to us is a Person. He desires to break through our disappointments and break through our fears with resurrection power. He knows that deep inside of us is a place that is prepared for His presence. These are times that His love breaks through and His power explodes within us. When we get a glimpse of Him, we break out of our hopeless prisons of fear and follow behind our King, the Breaker!

I am sure that when the Shunammite woman placed her dead son on the prophet's bed, she was extremely disappointed. She may have feared that this was the "will of God" and that the prophet would not come. Yet she pursued him and told everyone "It is well." She positioned herself above her fears and disappointments and determined to bring Elisha and the power of God home with her to that upper room. The place was prepared for a miracle.

As we prepare a place for the Lord to rest and abide in our lives, we can know that when we are faced with impossible situations, He will come and abide with us there. He will overtake our fears and disappointments with His wonderful presence and power.

— PRAYER —

Lord, it is my desire to consecrate myself and prepare a habitation for You. I need to experience Your power in my life so that I can break through to my destiny. You see the places of my heart that are shut and locked because of the pain of the past—the heartbreaks, the disappointments. You see the fear—I am afraid to open up. Please, Lord, break through to me in Your power. Lead me out and I will follow. Your power is greater than my limitations. Holy Spirit, please resurrect my dreams that I may receive the power to accomplish Your purposes for my life. Amen.

EIGHT

It's Time
for Transformation

When God gave our church the strategy of praise as a weapon of breakthrough (see chapter 5), we found that strongholds and mindsets were assaulted and brought down. Ed Silvoso, President of Harvest Evangelism and author of *That None Should Perish*, defines a stronghold as "a mindset impregnated with hopelessness that causes us to accept as unchangeable situations that we know are contrary to the will of God."[1] We discovered that "the weapons of our warfare are not of the flesh, but divinely powerful for the destruction of fortresses" (2 Corinthians 10:4). Those things that we believed to be unchangeable because of our hopelessness began to give way under the pressure of consistent praise. Destructive lifetime cycles were disrupted by the conquering power of His presence.

As we discussed in the previous chapter, the place of preparation and consecration can become a place of the miraculous. The Shunammite woman who had prepared an upper chamber for the prophet for his rest, later had direct access to the miraculous when she needed it. Her breakthrough was directly linked to her relationship with the prophet. We read in 2 Kings 4:20–37 that after her son died she placed the child in the upper chamber, shut the door, saddled her donkey and pursued Elisha.

Initially, the prophet sent his servant Gehazi with his staff to place upon the boy. This was not satisfactory to the desperate mother. She persisted and prevailed upon the prophet—that he, himself, must come. The prophet, moved with compassion, arose and went with her. As they were coming to the house, Gehazi met them and announced that he had no success and that the child remained lifeless. Even so, the woman was positioned for a breakthrough because she had prepared the way for it. She had ministered to the need of the prophet. She had developed a personal relationship with the man of God that moved him to follow after her and revive her son.

When we are hospitable and sensitive to God's presence, we are not only building a relationship with Him but we are building a place of future breakthroughs. I have found that the more I worship Him the less concerned and conscious I am about my needs and desires. There was a time a few years ago when my devotional times were simply worship. By the time I had finished pouring out my adoration upon Him and ministering to Him, I did not really have anything else to say. I did not even remember the prayer requests that I had planned to present.

One day the Lord said to me, *You can ask anything you want from Me.* I trembled in His presence. I sat quietly for a very long time; I could not even think of anything to ask. As I sat there, I realized that I had not requested anything personal from the Lord for about eighteen months. I felt so satisfied with Him it seemed that I needed nothing. I remembered that Solomon had asked for wisdom (see 1 Kings 3:9). I thought that must be the best thing to request because Solomon's request had pleased God (verse 10). But I felt the Holy Spirit nudge me sweetly and say, *He really wants to bless you—be specific.* And so I took a few days to ponder my request.

I came back to the Lord with one request for each of my family members. Within one or two months, each of those things came to pass. One of those requests could have taken years of intercession and counseling. God had moved speedily! I have found that as I worship Him and minister to His needs, my needs are met. In that place of intimate relationship, there is fullness. There is no lack. It is the ultimate breakthrough because it is the ultimate freedom!

Tommy Tenney tells the story of a friend of his who was so heavy that he was socially inhibited. The friend desired to visit the homes of his friends but their furniture was not made to hold his weight. He wept as he told Tommy of his desire for fellowship. He said that whenever he enters a house he looks around the room to see if it will be possible to stay.

In Hebrew, the word for *glory*, *kabod*, literally means "weightiness."[2] Tommy poses this question: "I wonder how many times the 'weighty glory' of God has visited us but not come in?"[3] He says that the reason God does not stay with us is that "we haven't built a mercy seat to hold the glory of God. There is no place for Him to sit! What is comfortable to you and [me] is not comfortable to the *kabod*, the weightiness of God. We are happy to sit in our comfortable spiritual recliners all day, but the seat of God, the mercy seat is a little different. It is the only seat on earth that can bear the weight of His glory and compel Him to come in and stay."[4]

How is it that we can build a mercy seat so that God will be at home with us? David found the secret to gaining God's abiding presence when he established worship "24 hours, 7 days a week" in a simple tent. And God promises a day will come when He will return and rebuild David's tabernacle (see Amos 9:11–12). David's tent contained the Ark of the Covenant and the literal mercy seat guarded by two golden cherubim. These cherubim faced each other over the seat of God. Could it be that God is asking us to be the guardians of His glorious presence today? By worshiping Him could it be possible that we are hosting His Holiness? As He rebuilds David's tabernacle within us—a house of worship—we through our worship are building a place for Him.

Tommy Tenney, in comparing us as worshipers to the cherubim above the mercy seat, says, "The way we can build a mercy seat is to take our positions as purified, 'beaten' worshippers. One problem is that God still requires mercy seat worshippers to be formed of gold tried in the fire (purified), conformed (beaten) into the image of perfection, and moved into the proper position of unity for worship. This speaks of purity, brokenness, and unity—the three components of true worship under the new covenant of the blood of Jesus."[5]

Thus, here is our next key: *The kind of enduring change that we are seeking is called transformation.* This is not temporary relief from life's circumstances, such as a vacation can bring. Rather, it is purposeful, progressive and eternal. When a caterpillar emerges from the cocoon as a butterfly, this is transformation. The butterfly will never again look like a caterpillar. How do we achieve this kind of change? By becoming a "spirit and truth" worshiper.

Transformation: A Lifestyle of Worship

To become such a worshiper, we must first recognize our great need. We must come to the end of our resources and ourselves and realize that the void within us will never be satisfied until we have connected heart to heart with our Creator and ultimately to His divine desires for our lives. David, "a man after [God's] own heart" (1 Samuel 13:14) and a true worshiper, discovered that earthly riches and the prominence of position and title paled in comparison to one thing: "One thing I have asked from the LORD, that I shall seek: that I may dwell in the house of the LORD all the days of my life, to behold the beauty of the LORD and to meditate in His temple" (Psalm 27:4). He came to God in worship immediately when God called him to divine fellowship.

To be such worshipers who enjoy true relationship with God, we must not only recognize our need but do something about it. We must decide to seek and pursue Him at all costs and to come when He calls. Worship is not something that can be scheduled and squeezed into our already busy lives. It must be our priority and purpose for living. Literally, David had become afflicted in his soul for the presence of God: "Remember, O LORD, on David's behalf, all his affliction; how he swore to the LORD and vowed to the Mighty One of Jacob, 'Surely I will not enter my house, nor lie on my bed; I will not give sleep to my eyes or slumber to my eyelids, until I find a place for the LORD, a dwelling place for the Mighty One of Jacob'" (Psalm 132:1–4).

Webster's Dictionary defines *affliction* as "continual pain, distress, grief, trouble, poverty, pressed down."[6] David was in a constant state of pain or distress in his great longing for the return of God's presence. He knew that nothing else would relieve his affliction. Could it be that David found a key that opens the door—the door of His presence and fellowship and also the door to our destinies—that no man can shut? Revelation 3:7 begins: "He who is holy, who is true, who has the key of David, who opens and no one will shut, and who shuts and no one opens. . . ." Maybe worship is "the key of David." When we worship, certain openings to the enemy of our souls are slammed shut and locked by the wonderful presence of the Lord.

David realized that worship is a lifestyle. He worshiped God in the good times and in the bad times. He worshiped as he went into battles and when he won victories. He worshiped when Saul was chasing him and seeking to kill him and he worshiped at the painful time of the death of his child. He worshiped God as he left behind his throne to his son who betrayed him. He worshiped God upon his deathbed. Yes, for David, worship was the key to living life in God's presence.

Worship for us must not be simply the musical portion of a church service but rather a divine connection. As we praise God with thankful hearts, we will be brought into His presence (see Psalm 100:4; 1 Thessalonians 5:18). Worship is then the response of our hearts to the One we behold. Paul states in 2 Corinthians 3:18 that as we look upon Him, the Spirit will change us into His image from glory to glory.

TRANSFORMATION:
THE WORSHIPERS HE SEEKS

In John 4:1–42, we read of one woman's transformation. She came to draw water—an ordinary daily chore—and encountered Jesus waiting at the well. In that life-changing encounter, she was thrust forward into her purpose.

In this story, Jesus pursued fellowship with someone that other religious leaders would have rejected. In verse 23 Jesus explained, "An hour is coming, and *now is*, when the true worshipers will worship the Father in spirit and truth; *for such people the Father seeks* to be His worshipers" (emphasis added). Even though she was a woman of questionable reputation and she was a Samaritan, Jesus desired to spend His time with her.

The woman was amazed that He would speak to her and ask for a drink of water because this violated Jewish tradition. Jesus saw not only the woman's present circumstances but her purpose—to be a worshiper. When Jesus spoke to her of "living water" she said, "Sir, You have nothing to draw with and the well is deep; where then do You get that living water?" (verse 11). Jesus responded that His water would quench the thirst and would become "a well of water springing up to eternal life" (verse 14). Of course the woman desired this eternal water, which would free her of her miserable chore of coming daily to draw water in the heat of the day!

At that point, Jesus began to dig the well within this woman's inner being. He, though He had "nothing to draw with," went to the depth of her soul and revealed the truth about her life. "You have correctly said, 'I have no husband'; for you have had five husbands, and the one whom you now have is not your husband; this you have said truly" (verses 17–18).

The woman then realized that this man was no ordinary rabbi but a prophet. In her hunger and thirst she asked Him the most important question in her heart. Her question was not about her own personal concerns or future; her question was about worship. She wanted to know the truth.

After Jesus revealed to her the heart of the Father for relationship with true worshipers, He told her the greatest secret of all. She was the first person to hear the news that He was the Messiah. The confession of Peter that Jesus was the Christ had not yet occurred.

What did Jesus see in this woman that He should make such a revelation? He saw someone who desired truth and who desired to worship. The woman immediately left her waterpot, a valued household possession, and "went into the city" with her message (verse 28): "From that city many of the Samaritans believed in Him because of the word of the woman who testified, 'He told me all the things that I have done'" (verse 39).

There was no song service, no sermon, no altar call, no special music. But . . . there was worship. When the woman allowed the entrance of the truth into her heart, she was free to be who she was created to be: a worshiper. Did she sing a song to Jesus? Did she fall on her knees in adoration? Did she give Him an offering? Even though these are all acceptable expressions of worship, none of them occurred that day. When she gave Him her life, she refreshed Him with the drink He had come seeking. When she left her waterpot and declared the news about Him to her city, she worshiped with her life.

David said, "Behold, You desire truth in the innermost being" (Psalm 51:6). When we, like the woman at the well, allow the truth to penetrate to the deepest places of our beings, a well will be dug. We are promised that out of those deep places will flow "rivers of living water" (John 7:38). The places that have been hidden and covered will suddenly burst forth in worship when the light of the truth sets us free. The Holy Spirit will then be unhindered to flow out of our lives in worship.

Hindrances to Transformation

Sometimes the greatest hindrances to personal revival and a lifestyle of worship are our own perceptions about ourselves. If the woman at the well had held on to her own reputation and identity instead of accepting His, she would have missed her moment. What if she had said, "No one in that town will listen to me. I have such a bad past. Besides, what if it doesn't last? I may never really be able to change. I've always been like this and I probably always will be." The apostle Paul exhorts us

> that, in reference to your former manner of life, you lay aside the old self, which is being corrupted in accordance with the lusts of deceit, and that you be renewed in the spirit of your mind, and put on the new self, which in the likeness of God has been created in righteousness and holiness of the truth.
>
> EPHESIANS 4:22–24

Some time back the Holy Spirit explained this principle to me. He said, *You must walk out of your history and step into your destiny.* History is the study of the past events. Many times we become inward in our focus and "study" the past and all that has affected us, both good and bad. Jesus is so committed to our destiny that He canceled our history at Calvary! "He has taken it *out of the way,* having nailed it to the cross" (Colossians 2:14, emphasis added). Dr. Fuchsia Pickett states, "When the Holy Spirit shines His light on the truth of God's word and we choose to obey Him completely, we are going to be delivered from the hindrances that keep us from worshiping in spirit and in truth."[7]

The fulfillment of our destinies is directly linked to the union of God's will and word and our timely obedience. This will require us to be alert and seize *kairos*—strategic moments—windows of opportunity to the next position. Being rightly positioned in relationship to God is critical to our promotion and advancement. This position is gained through a lifestyle of repentance and prompt obedience to the voice of the Lord. This lifestyle is worship.

Many times we fail to accept the historic power of the cross to deal with the past and, therefore, are left with a view of ourselves instead of the hope and destinies we have in Him! Dr. Pickett further states, "Worshipping God dethrones every usurper *(including our past)* that would demand our allegiance, perpetrate unbelief in our hearts or try to thwart the purposes of God for our lives. Enthroning God in our hearts deals a death blow to our self-nature, perhaps the greatest enemy to the will of God"[8] (emphasis added). In worship, we lay down our self-images—what we like about ourselves and what we do not like about ourselves—and we pursue Him and His divine image and nature. Our hope and our future are all in Him and His presence in our lives.

"IT IS FINISHED!"

Have you ever wished you could start all over? Do you ever look back longingly and say, "If only . . ."? The expression "Hindsight has 20/20 vision" is certainly true. Regret and shame have a powerful way of pulling us into the past. They are enemies to the future and they show no mercy. When Jesus said, "It is finished!" (John 19:30), not only was the suffering of the crucifixion over, but your past sins and mine were completely obliterated.

Jesus finished our pasts for us on Calvary! We cannot take hold of the future until we let go of the past. If you are willing to close yesterday's door by embracing what Jesus did on the cross, you will receive a double portion of the presence of God in exchange for your regrets and humiliation (see Isaiah 61:7).

Consider this: The Israelite women who left Egypt and followed Moses into the wilderness offered their mirrors to be used for the laver in the tabernacle (see Exodus 38:8). This was significant because a mirror was a treasured possession or symbol of their freedom from bondage. It was one of the spoils taken from their captivity. As an act of worship, women gave up the right to look at themselves for the greater purpose of looking upon God and serving Him. That which once reflected the image of a woman now reflected the fire of the sacrifice upon the altar.

Many times our own images of ourselves keep us from our destinies of serving God and reflecting Him. If we will stop gazing upon ourselves and our pasts and begin to behold Him, we will be transformed. The glory of the Lord will change us into His image as we look into the mirror of His Word (see 2 Corinthians 3:18).

God has a message for you today. He is declaring new things for your life. One definition of the word new is "not existing before."[9] The creative power of the Lord is about to do some things in your life that have never been done before!

Would you be willing to give Jesus your mirror—your image of yourself? Your past? If you will look upon His finished work of the cross, your life will reflect the fiery passion of His sacrifice. The past, with all of its pain, will lose its power; and you, like the woman at the well, will be "free to be all that He has destined you to be."[10]

TRUE WORSHIP

In Luke 7:36–50, we read of another woman who had to walk out of her history in order to seize her destiny. She had to rise out of her past and her reputation in order to accomplish her divine purpose. She had to keep her gaze upon Him in order to complete her heavenly assignment. On that day, she dared not gaze into her mirror at her own image or she would have failed. She exhibited true worship.

A true worshiper counts the cost and is unreservedly extravagant. This woman came to Jesus with her alabaster box filled with precious ointment. As she broke open the box in worshipful adoration, she broke through into the purpose of God for her life. Jesus honored her, an immoral woman in the eyes of the surrounding religious crowd, for her worship. In Jewish tradition such a box was usually a woman's dowry—to be broken and poured upon her husband on their wedding day. Once the seal was broken it could never again be sealed. This woman literally could have been spending her future in worshipful abandon.

A true worshiper loses the fear of man for the sake of the love of God. As the fragrance filled the room, the Pharisee who had invited Jesus was offended that He would allow such a woman to touch Him. The Breaker anointing is present upon extravagant, abandoned worship! We *break through* to new dimensions of His presence and break out of our past and the fear of man. As we break open our lives and pour ourselves out upon Him, He breaks us through to our destinies. Jesus said to this woman, "Your faith has saved you. Go in peace" (verse 50). She was no longer a slave to her history; now she had a new walk of destiny.

A true worshiper is forever transformed.

138

— PRAYER —

Lord, I pray for my friends that they will receive, even now, the Breaker anointing—the anointing that comes upon spirit and truth worshipers to bring forth transformation! May the sweet fragrance of their worshipful lives be pleasant to You. May their own identities be displaced by Yours. And may Your purposes suddenly be released upon them like a downpour of rain. In the name of Jesus, our Breaker. Amen.

NINE

SOWING WITH A VIEW

> *Sow with a view to righteousness, reap in accordance with kindness; break up your fallow ground, for it is time to seek the LORD until He comes to rain righteousness on you.*
>
> HOSEA 10:12

In the beginning of 2002, the Lord spoke prophetically to me of the generation that He is raising in this hour. He said to me: *I am raising up a new breed of prophetic people. They will be an earthshaking, groundbreaking, gate-opening, heaven-rending and glory-revealing generation! These are the ones who will seek My face.*

My first response was to let the Lord know that even though I am approaching fifty, I want to be a part of this new prophetic people. I had heard numerous ministers declare to young people that they were the "Joshua generation"—the ones who would go in and possess the land of promise. They would be bold conquerors who would gain the inheritance that the previous generation had failed to possess. Whenever I heard one of these messages, I would desperately cry out to the Lord to please let me come, too. I did not want to be left to die in the wilderness!

Finally, the truth dawned upon me that Joshua was in his eighties at the time he led the people into their inheritance. I rejoiced as the Lord reminded me of this in the beginning of 2002. I could be a part of the new breed of prophetic people! To God, a generation is not limited to a certain age group. This prophetic generation, from God's perspective, will be those people who have set their hearts on the same thing—to seek His face. To be a prophetic person simply means to be one who gains God's perspective on a matter and prays and declares it. In teaching us to pray, Jesus said, "Your kingdom come. Your will be done, on earth as it is in heaven" (Matthew 6:10).

Thus, our next key to change: *If we can gain heaven's will and perspective on any given situation, we can then pray for that perspective to become reality on earth.*

Jesus also taught that answers to prayer are released when two agree on earth about anything they may ask. He said, "It shall be done for them by My Father who is in heaven" (Matthew 18:19). From this we know that if two believers agree in faith on anything in His name, the power of God will be released into that situation. Can you imagine how powerful it could be to connect heaven's perspective to earth's reality by linking your heart in agreement with God Himself?

STRATEGY FOR PROPHETIC BREAKTHROUGH

The key to gaining God's perspective is to be positioned where He is. If I climb a mountain peak and gaze over the luscious landscape of the valley below, my view is much wider and more inclusive than if I sit inside my house and look at snapshots of the same valley. Or if someone who has been to the mountain peak describes to me how it looks from there, I can only try to imagine it. Similarly, if I limit my view of a situation to what I read in a book, hear from a sermon or gain from another person's comparable experience, I am earthbound in my perspective.

However, if I go to the mountain peak myself, I will be able to express with confidence the full view I have seen. It will not be secondhand information; it will be firsthand revelation.

This is why I believe that many of us find prayer time to be rather boring; we have not had the thrill of seeing things from God's perspective. We simply pray the information we have based upon the situations we are in. We hear sermons, read books, attend seminars and listen to tapes that tell us "how to" do most everything, but we have not personally encountered the One who is the answer. We apply spiritual formulas, follow prayer manuals and take the steps that will bring us into an overcoming position, but we have yet to go to the secret place, face to face with God, ourselves. When our human methods fail, we become hopeless about prayer and wonder why God does not do for us what He has done for others.

Some time ago I experienced a disappointing time in my prayer life. A man I respect immensely sent out a prayer calendar that would bring us out of our "wilderness wanderings" if we would pray, fast and declare the Scriptures printed there each day for several weeks. I was in a particularly dry time in my life and was excited to join this prayer strategy. At the end of the time, however, I had to admit, sadly, that nothing had changed. It was then that the Lord spoke to me and said, *Your faith was focused on the method and the anointing of the man. I have a strategy that is customized especially for you. If you seek* Me *and* My *ideas, you will discover that strategy and move into victory.*

There was nothing wrong with my friend's prayer strategy, but it was his and it worked for him, not me. I learned that I must seek the Lord and find *His* perspective if I was going to come out of my wilderness. I knew one thing for sure . . . I wanted out! As I sought Him, I found that the only way out is up.

> Who may *ascend* into the hill of the LORD? And who may stand in His holy place? He who has clean hands and a pure heart, who has not lifted up his soul to falsehood and has not sworn deceitfully. He shall receive a blessing from the LORD and righteousness from the God of his salvation. This is the generation of those who seek Him, who seek Your face—even Jacob.
>
> PSALM 24:3–6, EMPHASIS ADDED

David found, and relates in this psalm, that he could be positioned with God on His holy mountain when his hands were clean, his heart was pure and his soul was living in the truth. Today as we give our lives in daily repentance, we can stand clean through the redemptive power of the blood of Christ. Therefore, we can come boldly to the throne of grace with our requests. As we stand positioned in His presence, we gain heaven's perspective and can begin to pray powerful prophetic prayers—those that link heaven's Kingdom purposes to earth's needs. It is here on God's mountain that the Holy Spirit helps us and teaches us how to pray from His divine perspective.

> In the same way the Spirit also helps our weakness; for we do not know how to pray as we should, but the Spirit Himself intercedes for us with groanings too deep for

words; and He who searches the hearts knows what the mind of the Spirit is, because He intercedes for the saints according to the will of God. And we know that God causes all things to work together for good to those who love God, to those who are called according to His purpose.

ROMANS 8:26–28

Have you ever felt speechless before God? Isn't it amazing that the Holy Spirit can take even our groans and turn them into powerful intercession? He will pray God's perspective and purposes through us as we yield to Him. And God will work *all* things together for good!

Our part as a prophetic people is to position ourselves in God's presence, gain His perspective and pray in agreement with His purposes. God's response is to release the power to bring His Kingdom to earth. The divine connection of agreement with God is the secret to the release of His power to His people. If I have a lamp and I never plug it in to the power source, it will never accomplish its purpose. It will have all of the potential for giving light in its wiring, but it will be of little use without the necessary electricity. So it is with us. If we do not connect to heaven's perspective, we will not radiate heaven's power in our situations. Our potential for fulfilling our dreams and embracing God's plans for us will be limited.

If we will have faith for the things that seem impossible, we must see that which is invisible. Paul said, "We look not at the things which are seen, but at the things which are not seen; for the things which are seen are temporal, but the things which are not seen are eternal" (2 Corinthians 4:18). John, the revelator, said that he heard a voice like the sound of a trumpet, which said, "Come up here, and I will show you what must take place after these things" (Revelation 4:1). I believe the

145

Lord is still calling His people to come to where He is so that He can reveal to us what is to come. This is why we must "press on toward the goal for the prize of the *upward* call of God in Christ Jesus" (Philippians 3:14, emphasis added).

ENLIGHTENED EYES

One of the people who have greatly influenced my life, and whom I have quoted in this book, is Dr. Fuchsia Pickett. Dr. Pickett holds two earned doctorates in theology. She has taught seminary classes and written numerous books. Besides her vast knowledge of the Scriptures, she has a deep river of revelation that flows continually from her personal times in God's presence.

Often I would express to her how much I wanted that kind of revelation. She would respond, "You can go get it the same place I did. You can have as much of God as you want." She did not try to meet my need but pointed me in the direction of the mountain of God. She challenged me to begin my own climb. She also encouraged me to read and pray the following passage with my whole heart, believing that He would grant my request. I knew that this was more than another "formula" because my heart leapt within me as I sensed that I was going to encounter God, the Source of revelation.

[I pray] that the God of our Lord Jesus Christ, the Father of glory, may give to you a spirit of wisdom and of revelation in the knowledge of Him. I pray that the eyes of your heart may be *enlightened*, that you will know what is the hope of His calling, what are the riches of the glory of His inheritance in the saints, and what is

the surpassing greatness of His power toward us who
believe.

EPHESIANS 1:17–19, EMPHASIS ADDED

As I came into God's presence, praying that I could have
His perspective, my view began to change. I began to see
things from a whole new vantage point. Things that had
seemed insurmountable and unchangeable began to shrink
as I ascended higher and higher into God's way of thinking.
In my study of the passage, I discovered the Greek meaning
for *enlightened*. The word *photizo* is actually the root of our
English word *photograph*. The Greek meaning is "to imbue
with saving knowledge, to give light or to shine, to bring to
light."[1] I wondered why such a word was used to describe a
photograph. I spoke with someone who has knowledge of
cameras to get some understanding. When a photograph is
taken, the shutter of the camera opens, light shoots in and
the image is transferred to light-sensitive paper. That image
on the paper is the photograph. As I applied this to the passage, I realized that the light of God's presence and divine
perspective comes into my heart (if it is light sensitive!) and
transfers His image to my life.

Maybe this could explain why a person like Moses, an
insecure stuttering shepherd, was transformed into a
powerful deliverer of a nation. Light must have come from
the burning bush into the darkness of his doubting heart.
He must have received the revelation of God's perspective
to empower him to fulfill his destiny. We know that Moses'
prayer life was anything but boring and ordinary! He would
return from the mountain of God or the tent of meeting
with his face shining.

If we, like Moses, can get our eyes off of ourselves and
our situations and upon God's face, we too will have a
prayer life that changes things. We will be an earthshak-

ing, groundbreaking, gate-opening, heaven-rending and glory-revealing generation! Our perspectives will not be limited to our personal experiences, opinions or *self-images*, but we will have His view and His authority when we pray. As we position ourselves in His glorious presence, the shutter of our souls will open, His light will enter and an image will be transferred to our hearts.

Paul said, "We all, with unveiled face, beholding as in a mirror the glory of the Lord, are being transformed *into the same image* from glory to glory, just as from the Lord, the Spirit" (2 Corinthians 3:18, emphasis added). Paul's encounter with God's light had blinded his natural eyes and yet it had enlightened the eyes of his heart. He was transformed from a persecutor of the Church to an anointed apostle. His image was changed as a result of the changed perspective he had gained that day on the road to Damascus (see Acts 9). Throughout the epistles we read the prophetic prayers and messages of Paul, who saw people and situations in the Spirit even though he was usually in a different geographical location. His viewpoint from God's mountain was unobstructed and he prayed and ministered powerfully because of it.

What would have happened if Paul had refused to let go of the image of his past life? Suppose he had lived in condemnation, guilt and shame because of what he had done to the Church in his days of darkness. If he had kept his own perspective, he would never have become the apostle that God had called him to be. He declared that he was pressing on, "forgetting what lies behind and reaching forward to what lies ahead" (Philippians 3:13). In that forward reach he must have made many trips to the mountain of God to be reminded of the Lord's perspective.

Is that what you need to do in order to walk out of your history and step into your destiny? Do you need to gain

God's perspective so that you can pray prophetically and powerfully and see things change? Why not make the climb? The view is great from there! When heaven's Kingdom comes to earth, the earth shakes, the ground breaks, the gates open and the glory is revealed. Now that is powerful prayer!

Sowing Seeds of Prayer

Sow with a view to righteousness, reap in accordance with kindness; break up your fallow ground, for it is time to seek the LORD until He comes to rain righteousness on you.

Hosea 10:12

Prophetic prayer that proceeds from God's presence sows into the heavens. The heavens then rain down His promised righteousness onto the ground of our lives.

When farmers are desperate for rain, they often hire pilots to "seed" the clouds. The airplanes are loaded with a certain chemical and release it into the clouds, which makes them heavy. The clouds can no longer hold the rain because of the weightiness caused by the seeding. As a result, rain is released and crops are revived. As we sow our seeds of prophetic prayers into the heavens, the weight of these prayers creates pressure in the spiritual realm, which releases God's power from heaven to earth!

I have seen this illustrated many times in my own prayer life. One example involved a teenage girl, whom I will call Marci. She attended a church we pastored and caused her parents much grief by the choices she made. She would enter the Sunday morning service dressed in a very short, tight skirt and low-cut top. She would make her entrance in the middle of the worship time, walking all the way to the front of the church. She would then proceed to push her way past a few teenage boys to get to the place she intended to sit.

This particular disruption went on for several weeks and some "concerned" church members approached me. That is to say, they were not concerned about Marci or her condition but about the distraction she was to others. They strongly suggested that I do something about it. I asked the Lord for His perspective on this young woman. He gave me His perspective and told me to "sow with a view" regarding her.

I began to pray consistently what God had shown me about Marci. Then, one Sunday morning I felt it was time for the rain of His presence to fall upon her life. I said to her, "Marci, you are so beautiful. I am so blessed every time I see you! The Lord loves you so much and I am so excited to *see* all He is doing in your life. You are such an awesome woman of God and you shine with His light. I am so proud of you and so glad to *see* you pursuing God's plan for your life." Marci crumbled into tears, fell into my arms and within minutes had recommitted her life to the Lord. She later told me that the love of God had conquered all of her defenses and had drawn her back to Him that day.

When God called Peter to minister to Cornelius and the other Gentiles, He gave him heaven's perspective. He answered Peter's arguments by declaring, "What God *has cleansed* [has already done], no longer consider unholy" (Acts 10:15, emphasis added). Before the Gospel had even been preached to Cornelius and his household, God declared them to be cleansed.

This is the principle I applied to Marci. In prayer I declared God's perspective about her instead of my own. If I had prayed my way, I would have said:

God, please do something with Marci. She is really going down the wrong path. The way she's headed she will probably end up dead. So, You have to do something! Besides, her parents are so heartbroken and our church people are getting upset. Lord, if You don't do something soon, she could affect the whole youth group in a negative way. So, please change her.

After I had God's perspective, my prayers for Marci went something like this:

Lord, I thank You for Marci. I know that the finished work of Calvary is enough for her. I thank You for her deliverance, salvation and transformation. I praise You that You have created her so beautifully and placed Your favor upon her. Thank You, Lord, that Your presence and purposes for her life will rain down upon her and wash away her past. Thank You that You have given her a future and a hope as she turns back to You, even now!

God declares "the end from the beginning, and from ancient times things which have not been done, saying, 'My purpose will be established, and I will accomplish all My good pleasure'" (Isaiah 46:10). Aren't you glad that God stands in the place of your future fulfillment and sows with a view toward righteousness about you? I believe that He is looking for a new breed of prophetic people who will join with Him and pray in agreement with His perspective so that the rain of righteousness can pour down upon our lives and upon others' lives.

When Jesus was stretched out between heaven and earth on the cross, He looked through the ages and saw you. He saw you saved, delivered, healed and fulfilled. His death portrays to us the ultimate prophetic prayer. Suspended between the sin and darkness of the earth and the purposes and plans of heaven, He established our breakthrough. He sowed with a view.

— PRAYER —

Lord Jesus, thank You for seeing me from the place of Your finished work on Calvary. I desire to be a part of the new breed who pray Your perspective and establish Your Kingdom's purposes on the earth. As I ascend Your holy mountain in repentance and worship, please enlighten my eyes. I need Your image to displace my own. I am committed to the climb. Amen.

TEN

THE ROAR OF THE LION

Surely the Lord GOD does nothing unless He reveals His secret counsel to His servants the prophets. A lion has roared! Who will not fear? The Lord GOD has spoken! Who can but prophesy?

AMOS 3:7–8

But one who prophesies speaks to men for edification and exhortation and consolation.

1 CORINTHIANS 14:3

I stood impatiently waiting as Dr. Bill Hamon prayed and prophesied over every pastor in the line. It seemed that Dan and I had been there forever. Actually it had been an hour and a half and we were the last ones in line.

I was not so sure what I thought of personal prophecy; I was at the meeting at the insistence of our friends. They had said they were certain that Dr. Hamon would have a prophetic word for us. He had a word for every pastor in the place! By this time, it was one o'clock in the morning and I wondered why we had ever consented to this.

I whispered to my husband, "Maybe we should just leave. It's so late and we're tired." Before Dan could answer me, Dr. Hamon stood in front of us. I stood in awe as he prophesied the secret desires of my heart that only God knew. I was so encouraged and hope for my future sprang up in my soul. From that moment, it seemed that everything regarding my personal destiny was accelerated. It was as though I had been on the launching pad and needed my fuse to be lit. That prophecy launched me!

FROM PRAYER TO PROCLAMATIONS

Part of the word of the Lord that was given to me that night was that God would use me to prophesy. He said that I was called as a prophet to the nations. This part of the word was not encouraging. In fact, it was terrifying because I did not feel comfortable even praying in front of people, much less prophesying. I would do it because of my role as a pastor's wife, but I was very content to keep my prayers in a private place with God.

Basically, I have always been a shy person. Granted, as I have mentioned, as a child I had been visited by the Lord and had desired to "be a preacher when I grow up." I guess that the idea of facing real people with my message instead of Betsy Wetsy, Tiny Tears, Chatty Cathy and the other dolls of my childhood was not so appealing. Yet, something had been ignited inside of me and was stirred again when Dr. Hamon laid his hands on me and prophesied. I had to admit to myself that even though I was terrified, at the same time I was excited to discover all this would mean for me.

There are numerous books written on this subject such as Dr. Hamon's *Prophets and Personal Prophecy* and Cindy Jacobs' *The Voice of God*. These books and others explain the gift of prophecy in excellent detail. My purpose, however, for this chapter is to encourage you to "desire earnestly" (1 Corinthians 14:1) to prophesy.

After the time of personal ministry stirred me to pursue my calling, I began a prophetic journey that has taught me the power of anointed proclamations to bring breakthroughs. This is our next key: *I have learned that as we gain God's perspective on a situation and begin to pray prophetically (sowing with a view), oftentimes those prayers will turn into proclamations. Those proclamations or prophetic declarations are anointed by the Holy Spirit and are powerful weapons of breakthrough.*

I have mentioned how throughout Jesus' ministry He would go aside to pray to the Father, often all night. Scripture also tells repeatedly of His proclamations such as: "I say to you, get up, and pick up your stretcher and go home" (Luke 5:24) or "Lazarus, come forth" (John 11:43). In the place of prayer with the Father, Jesus received perspective and direction. He returned to the people with powerful proclamations of healing and deliverance.

Prophecy in its purest definition simply means to speak for God. Paul exhorted his spiritual son Timothy to wage effective warfare using the prophecies that had been given concerning him (see 1 Timothy 1:18). When we have spent time with God in prayer to gain His perspective and direction, we too can proclaim what He has said over our lives and win the war that wages against fulfilling our destinies.

THE ROAR OF THE LION

A few years ago I went on an African safari. I had just finished some ministry assignments and we ended our trip with this extraordinary adventure. I was amazed to see the lions lying peacefully in the brush with zebras and impalas grazing nearby. I wondered aloud why they were not afraid of the ones who normally would have eaten them for dinner. Our guide explained that the lions had recently eaten and that they would fast for about two weeks until it was time to eat again. When that time came, the lions would roar and begin their hunt. Until then, life for the other animals was relatively safe.

The prophet Amos compares the proclaimed word of the Lord to the roar of a lion. When the Lord uses us to prophesy—or speak for Him—there is a change in the atmosphere. Just as the lion's roar sends forth an alert and causes the animals to flee, so the prophetic proclamation puts our enemy, the devil, on the run! There is a breakthrough, a change over the situation or person receiving the word of the Lord because the opposition is removed by His power.

In my personal situation, I found that when the Lord spoke through me to declare His word, my shyness seemed to disappear. I had a new sense of authority and could feel the strength of the Lord empowering me as I yielded myself to Him. As well, I began to see significant changes come into the lives of people and their circumstances as I prophesied. The sound of triumph and the sound of overcoming is in the roar of the Lion of the tribe of Judah (see Revelation 5:5). When He roars, things will change!

He will roar like a lion; indeed He will roar and His sons will come trembling.

HOSEA 11:10

The LORD roars from Zion and utters His voice from Jerusalem, and the heavens and the earth tremble.

JOEL 3:16

The wicked flee when no one is pursuing, but the righteous are bold as a lion.

PROVERBS 28:1

THE AUTHORITY OF GOD'S VOICE

The voice of the LORD is upon the waters; the God of glory thunders, the LORD is over many waters. The voice of the LORD is powerful, the voice of the LORD is majestic. The voice of the LORD breaks the cedars; yes, the LORD breaks in pieces the cedars of Lebanon. He makes Lebanon skip like a calf, and Sirion like a young wild ox. The voice of the LORD hews out flames of fire. The voice of the LORD shakes the wilderness; the LORD shakes the wilderness of Kadesh. The voice of the LORD makes the deer to calve and strips the forests bare; and in His temple everything says, "Glory!"

PSALM 29:3–9

When we begin to speak for God, or prophesy, the Lord places His authority upon our voices and upon the words we declare. What an awesome privilege and responsibility He has given to us, His Church! We literally find ourselves standing as His representatives when we speak for Him. We are "ambassadors for Christ" (2 Corinthians 5:20).

An ambassador is one who represents the interests of his leader and nation. He lives in a foreign land and he communicates the concerns of those who sent him. He demonstrates by his words and actions the way things are done in his country. He is in constant communication with his home base, receiving current information and direction. He then acts as the voice for his leader. He has been chosen because of his loyalty and integrity to his country. As

157

Christ's ambassadors, the same is true of us. He trusts us to be in continual communication with Him (prayer) and then to speak for Him what we have heard (prophecy).

No one is able to prophesy perfectly, "for we know in part and we prophesy in part" (1 Corinthians 13:9). No one can know the totality of the depth and height of God's mind on any matter, except the Holy Spirit (see 1 Corinthians 2:9–11). We are never able to express completely what is in the vastness of God's heart. However, we can depend on the Holy Spirit to help us give voice to the "part" God has given us. He is the One who anoints us and empowers us with God's authority.

> The Spirit of the Lord GOD is upon me, because the LORD has anointed me to bring good news to the afflicted; He has sent me to bind up the brokenhearted, to proclaim liberty to captives and freedom to prisoners; to proclaim the favorable year of the LORD and the day of vengeance of our God; to comfort all who mourn, to grant those who mourn in Zion, giving them a garland instead of ashes, the oil of gladness instead of mourning, the mantle of praise instead of a spirit of fainting. So they will be called oaks of righteousness, the planting of the LORD, that He may be glorified.
>
> ISAIAH 61:1–3

When the Spirit of the Lord anoints us to proclaim the Good News, a powerful exchange takes place. There is an exchange of:

- Captivity and bondage for liberty and freedom
- Mourning for comfort and gladness
- Fainting or heaviness of heart for a garment of praise

- An old identity for a new identity of permanence and stability in God's presence that glorifies Him.

The phrase *freedom to prisoners* means "an opening to those who are bound."[1] When we speak with the Spirit's anointing, we are making a way or pointing to the door of breakthrough for those who are bound. If a person is trapped in a burning building and cannot find the way out because of the smoke, a fireman may lead him out with his voice. He may not be able to reach the victim or be visible to him but he can shout, "Come this way! The exit is over here!" The same thing happens when we stand at the threshold of breakthrough and shout with God's authority and anointing, "Come this way! Follow my voice to the opening of breakthrough!" Jesus said as He sent forth the seventy, "The one who listens to you listens to Me" (Luke 10:16).

RIVERS OF LIVING WATER

According to the prophet Ezekiel and John, the revelator, the voice of the Lord is "like the sound of abundant [or many] waters" (Ezekiel 1:24; Revelation 1:15; 14:2). Look now at John's description of the worshipers in heaven: "Then I heard something like the voice of a great multitude and like the *sound of many waters* and like the sound of mighty peals of thunder, saying, 'Hallelujah! For the Lord our God, the Almighty, reigns'" (Revelation 19:6, emphasis added).

It appears that the Lord's voice and His people's voices have the same sound! Jesus declared that "If anyone is thirsty, let him come to Me and drink. He who believes in Me, as the Scripture said, 'From his innermost being will flow rivers of living water'" (John 7:37–38). In this passage Jesus was speaking of the Holy Spirit, who would come after He was glorified (see verse 39). The Lord's desire is for His Spirit to have a free flow in the life of every believer. If the river of God, which flows from His throne, is within us, what an incredible source of life and power we possess! Can you imagine what would happen if that living water began to flow over the landscape of our lives and the lives of others? Suppose we all began to let God's voice speak through us to declare His plans and purposes. Breakthroughs would be inevitable!

You may be wondering how to do this because you want to speak for God and see changes happen for yourself and for others. The prophet Isaiah speaks of a day when the wilderness will rejoice and the desert will blossom. In that day he says that the glory and the majesty of the Lord will be seen (see Isaiah 35:1–2). He then gives us the secret to this transformation:

> Encourage the exhausted, and strengthen the feeble. *Say* to those with anxious heart, "Take courage, fear not. Behold, your God will come with vengeance; the recompense of God will come, but He will save you."
>
> VERSES 3–4, EMPHASIS ADDED

Prophesying does not have to be complicated, deep and mystical. I often tell those I train that they do not need a microphone and they do not have to speak in King James' English. You do not have to shout or place your hands on people's heads. You simply need to pray and then "say" what God wants to say. You do not have to be in a church building to prophesy. You can speak for God at the grocery store, your place of business, the gas station or your school. You just need to let His river flow from your life to the wilderness places of those around you. This changes everything! "Everything will live where the river goes" (Ezekiel 47:9).

Thus, you might be led to say to an exhausted person, "I see how tired you are. Just remember the Lord is with you. He will help you!" You might be led to say to someone who is afraid, "Don't worry. You can trust God. He will take care of it!" Suppose a person has been treated unfairly or has an upcoming legal matter that is pressing him? You may hear God's heart on the matter and declare, "The Lord is just and He will defend you and take up your cause."

MIRACLES IN THE DESERT

As we say these things, the realm of the supernatural begins to open up and God's word breaks through.

> Then the eyes of the blind will be opened and the ears of the deaf will be unstopped. Then the lame will leap like a deer, and the tongue of the mute will shout for joy. For *waters will break forth in the wilderness* and streams in the [desert].
>
> ISAIAH 35:5–6, EMPHASIS ADDED

The voice of the Lord is truly powerful. It transforms lives and brings forth God's purposes. How awesome it is to realize His voice resides in us!

> But if the Spirit of Him who raised Jesus from the dead dwells in you, He who raised Christ Jesus from the dead will also give life to your mortal bodies through His Spirit who dwells in you.
>
> ROMANS 8:11

— PRAYER —

Lord, teach me how to speak for You. Teach me to release Your life through my life. May the rivers within me break forth and water the wilderness places of many so that miraculous transformations will be the result. Lord, especially, I ask You to begin with my wilderness—the places that need to be changed for Your glory. Help me to speak over my life what You are saying instead of my own opinions. Use my voice for breakthrough! Amen.

ELEVEN

HARVEST GLORY

> *"Arise, shine; for your light has come, and the glory of the Lord has risen upon you. For behold, darkness will cover the earth and deep darkness the peoples; but the Lord will rise upon you and His glory will appear upon you. Nations will come to your light, and kings to the brightness of your rising."*
>
> ISAIAH 60:1–3

In the introduction to this book, I said that it is intended for a prophetic people—those pregnant with the purposes of God. These people carry in their spiritual wombs not only personal destiny but corporate revival!

At the time of this writing my daughter Kari is pregnant with her first child, Noah. I have enjoyed watching her pregnancy through spiritual eyes. Through it I have been learning some principles of carrying God's plan for our lives. I watch as Kari walks with a new kind of walk as her body adjusts to the extra weight of the baby. I have noticed that once simple tasks, such as bending over or getting out of a chair, now are not so simple. She says that she can never seem to get comfortable. Yesterday she called me on the phone frustrated with her "clumsiness." She had knocked over a display at the grocery store!

To see the sparkle in her eye the first time she felt movement was priceless. She loves making plans for Noah's room and buying baby things. Sometimes she works to the point of exhaustion making preparations. I have told her that this is "nesting." She says that she "can't wait" until her delivery—but she will. It has been a blessing to watch her husband, Tim, patiently get whatever food for her that her cravings demand. He sat with her through many days of morning sickness and even joined her in "not feeling so good." When Kari had a doctor's visit, Tim stepped on the scale to see how much he had gained too. Together, they will do this!

I have told Kari that there is a point during labor when she will feel like changing her mind, but her body will stay committed to the process. This point is called transition. It is during transition that it will be time to begin to push. Once Noah is born, Tim and Kari will say it was worth it all! Their home and their lives will never be the same.

I am sure that as you approach your delivery date, you, too, may not be able to "get comfortable." Your pregnant condition has changed your walk and things may not seem to be as easy as they used to be before you were in this condition. You have cravings that are unexplainable and it seems as though you have been "preparing" forever! Waiting seems to be getting more and more difficult, especially since you can feel the stirring of life within you. Jesus patiently helps you, encouraging you day by day, providing what you need. He identifies very personally with us because He understands what it is like to wait for fulfillment.

As you come to the "appointed time," you can apply the principles of breakthrough that will bring you through the transition and to delivery. It will be the dawning of a new day! It will be a breakthrough of God's destiny for your life.

Just as you personally will enter into a new day of revival and fulfillment, so will the Church experience a corporate birthing of its purpose. The psalmist speaks of a volunteer army that will come forth from the womb of the dawn, clothed in holiness in the day of His power (see Psalm 110:3). The prophet Hosea called this "the third day" or the day of God's raising up His people.

> "Come, let us return to the LORD. For He has torn us, but He will heal us; He has wounded us, but He will bandage us. He will revive us after two days; He will raise us up on *the third day*, that we may live before Him. So let us know, let us press on to know the LORD. His going forth is as certain as the dawn; and He will come to us like the rain, like the spring rain watering the earth."
>
> HOSEA 6:1–3, EMPHASIS ADDED

If a day with God is like a thousand years (see 2 Peter 3:8), we are now beginning the "third day" of the history of the world. In this day, we will "live before Him." We will not go in and out of the presence of the Lord, but we will find ourselves abiding at all times in Him. It is from this place of glorious fellowship that the Bride will emerge without spot or wrinkle for the entire world to see.

A NEW DAY DAWNS: THE THIRD DAY

Throughout Scripture, we can see prophetic pictures or foreshadowing of the third day. Just as Hosea called the people to return to the Lord to prepare for the coming day, Moses instructed his people to "wash their garments; and let them be ready for the third day, for on the third day the LORD will come down on Mount Sinai in the sight of all the people" (Exodus 19:10–11). *It is time* for us, God's people, to consecrate ourselves and prepare for a very tangible visitation of God. We are promised that a day will come when His glory shall be revealed in such a way that "all flesh will see it together" (Isaiah 40:5).

On the third day, David received the word from the Lord to pursue his enemy: "For you will surely overtake them, and you will surely rescue all [his family and possessions that had been stolen]" (1 Samuel 30:8). He acted on the word of the Lord and recovered all the spoil and brought back his family. *It is time*, in this third day, to pursue and recover our families and all that the enemy has stolen in past seasons. There will especially be an anointing for the return of prodigal children. They are created for His glory and so *it is time* for their return (see Isaiah 43:5–7). The third day has a prophetic sound of the returning of the backslidden. The Breaker anointing is rising in this hour to break through the places of bondage that have been holding our loved ones in captivity! *It is time for restoration!*

Ezra reported of the joyful third day in which the rebuilding of the Temple was completed (see Ezra 6:15–16). Today, God's prophets are declaring that *it is time* for the good work that God has started in us to be completed, which means to be matured and fulfilled. The Lord is calling us to be fitted together into His building of lively stones so that we can house His glory (see 1 Peter 2:5). *It is time for unity!*

It was on the third day that Esther, after a time of fasting, gained the favor of the king, which resulted in the deliverance of her people and the destruction of their enemy (see Esther 5:1). *It is time* for those who have humbly submitted to the processes of preparation to be positioned in favor. An anointing and authority will be upon them for strategic prayer and intercession that will have an impact on nations with deliverance from destruction. *It is time for favor!*

On the third day, Jesus manifested His glory for the first time by turning water into wine at the wedding feast in Cana of Galilee. When the wine ran out, it could have been an extremely embarrassing situation for the host, but Jesus intervened by turning ordinary water into extraordinary wine (see John 2:1–11). Today, as the wedding feast is being prepared, the Church will experience the coming forth of new wine. The crushing, humiliating things we have experienced will be touched by Jesus' glory and will become a source of fruitful ministry. That which Satan has meant for our destruction will be turned to good. In this third day, the water of the Word that is within us will take on the taste of exquisite wine. That which has been ordinary and natural will become extraordinary and supernatural! There will be a fresh anointing of revelation upon the Word. *It is time for fruitfulness!*

The most significant scriptural event that happened on the third day was the resurrection of Jesus. In the dawning of this new day, there will be a breakthrough of God's power, which will raise up Jesus and His Church for all to see. Signs and wonders will be released in unprecedented measure through the Church. *It is time for miracles!*

IT IS TIME FOR CHANGE

He is the sole expression of the glory of God—the Light-being, the out-raying [or radiance] of the divine—and He is the perfect imprint and very image of [God's] nature, upholding and maintaining and guiding and propelling the universe by His mighty word of power.

HEBREWS 1:3, AMP

The purpose of this book has been to present keys to spiritual breakthroughs so that true change can happen in our lives and ministries. We are a people who have come to the end of ourselves and have desperately cried out for deliverance from sameness. Change is defined as "to cause to be different, to transform, to transition, to replace, to exchange for another."[1] We recognize that *it is time* for things to be different and we realize that we are in transition and coming into transformation. Our lives are being replaced and exchanged for the life of Christ as we embrace the cross daily.

As we take the keys to spiritual breakthrough and begin to use them, we must remember that our first and primary purpose is to apply them to our own lives. Change must start with me and it must start with you. *It is time* for me to change. *It is time* for you to change. We are promised that as we draw near and behold Him and look in the mirror of His Word, we will be "transformed into the same image from glory to glory, just as from the Lord, the Spirit" (2 Corinthians 3:18). *It is time for transformation!* As we come closer to Jesus, the sole expression of God's glory, we will begin to look like Him. *"He will raise us up on the third day"* (Hosea 6:2, emphasis added).

As we, the Church, are changed more and more into His image, there will be a rising of His presence in our lives that will be evident to all. The light of God's glory has been placed within us as a gift to those around us.

For God, who said, "Light shall shine out of darkness," is the One who has shone in our hearts to give the Light

168

of the knowledge of the glory of God in the face of Christ. But we have this treasure in earthen vessels, so that the surpassing greatness of the power will be of God and not from ourselves.

2 CORINTHIANS 4:6–7

As the light of God's truth and presence grows brighter and brighter in us, our vessels will break open with the intensity of His great love and power. The Lord's appearing upon His people will be the greatest evangelistic tool of the last days. Jesus admonished us saying, "Let your light shine before men in such a way that they may see your good works, and glorify your Father who is in heaven" (Matthew 5:16). Our Father is the "Father of lights" (James 1:17) and He covers Himself with light as a garment (Psalm 104:2). We, His children, shall wear the garment of His light—His glory—as we look to Him to clothe us. We are called to "Arise, shine; for your light has come, and the glory of the LORD has risen upon you" (Isaiah 60:1). We shall be raised up to shine with God's magnificent glory. The result will be the final harvest.

"NATIONS WILL COME TO YOUR LIGHT"

"For behold, darkness will cover the earth and deep darkness the peoples; but the LORD will rise upon you and His glory will appear upon you. Nations will come to your light, and kings to the brightness of your rising."

ISAIAH 60:2–3

When I was a small child, my parents took me to Carlsbad Caverns to see this gorgeous demonstration of God's handiwork. Hidden deep in the darkness are castles and treasures formed by the mixture of hydrogen sulfite gases and the ground waters seeping through cracks in the rocks. Slowly throughout the ages, by this process, the finger of God made the beautiful formations. Tourists can visit the caverns because man has made well-lit paths throughout them.

At one point on the tour, the ranger had everyone sit down on benches. He then had all the lights turned off. The darkness is indescribable. I remember holding my hand in front of my face and being unable to see it. I began to cry, "I can't find me!" My dad held me close and assured me that in one short minute there would be light and then I would find me. The ranger then lit a match. It seemed to light up the entire area. I said, "Let's stay with him, Daddy."

In these last days, a cover of increasing darkness has come down upon our world from the forces of evil. The darkness is growing darker, hiding the beauty of our world more and more. Many have lost the sense of the wonder of life and the innocence of days gone by. They have become deeply depressed and oppressed looking for comfort in entertainment, short-lived relationships and various addictions. Feelings of insecurity and overwhelming fear almost paralyze many. It seems that for some, life, in general, has lost its vibrancy and zest as people merely exist from day to day. People are crying out of the darkness, "Help me! I can't find myself."

The arising, glorious Church will draw them to the Light Bearer, Himself. The brightness of our rising will attract the lost and bring them out of darkness and into His marvelous light. The most magnificent change that we will ever see will be when entire nations return to the Lord. "For the earth will be filled with the knowledge of the glory of the LORD, as the waters cover the sea" (Habakkuk 2:14).

Hidden in the darkness of sin are great treasures destined to be redeemed by the power of the blood of Jesus. Someone just needs to shine. As the knowledge of the Lord's glory invades the lives of the lost, the Good News will spread rapidly, swallowing up the covering of darkness upon the earth. God swore in an oath to Moses: "Indeed, as I live, all the earth will be filled with the glory of the LORD" (Numbers 14:21). The Lord has determined to fulfill His Word and bring the ultimate breakthrough of all time through His shining, glorious Church.

God's most outstanding plan for change is the coming radiance of His glory emanating through you and the rest of His Church to illuminate our darkened world, transforming it to His purposes. Central to all of the spiritual keys to breakthrough is a common simple cry. It is at the very core of the message of change.

I wonder if you would like to join with me in the age-old cry of the dissatisfied. The cry for the ultimate change that penetrates the darkness of the soul is one of homesickness. It is a cry that will bring transformation not only to you and to me but to our world. The lovesick cry of the Bride will culminate in the splitting of the heavens and our faith shall be made sight. Until that final day we cry: "I pray You, show me Your glory!" (Exodus 33:18).

NOTES

Chapter 1: "Who Touched Me?"

1. Before I relate this life-changing dream to you, let me say that I understand that not all dreams are spiritual and that they must be evaluated according to the Word of God. Having said that, we also understand that God promised He would speak to us in dreams and visions (see Acts 2:17). The Scriptures are filled with examples of people who received divine revelation from God in this way.

Chapter 2: Enemies of Change

1. Sue Curran, *I Saw Satan Fall Like Lightning* (Lake Mary, Fla.: Creation House Publishers, 1998), p. 20.

Chapter 3: Divine Dissatisfaction

1. John Kilpatrick, *When the Heavens Are Brass* (Shippensburg, Pa.: Destiny Image Publishers, Inc., 1997), p. xi.

2. Tommy Tenney, *The God Catchers* (Nashville: Thomas Nelson Publishers, 2000), p. 101.

Chapter 4: God's Favor

1. Tommy Tenney, *God's Favorite House* (Shippensburg, Pa.: Destiny Image Publishers, Inc., 1999), p. 31.

2. For more information regarding this subject see the book by Dr. Iverna Tompkins and Dr. Dianne McIntosh, *Fearless Parenting—Handle with Love* (Plainsfield, N.J.: Bridge Logo Publishers, 1996).

3. James Strong, *Strong's Exhaustive Concordance of the Bible* (Peabody, Mass.: Hendrickson Publishers, n.d.), *meta* (G#3326) and *noieo* (G#3539).

4. Dutch Sheets, *The River of God* (Ventura, Calif.: Renew Books, A Division of Gospel Light, 1998), p. 104.

5. Ibid., p. 90.

6. Ibid., p. 109.

7. M. Basilea Schlink, *Repentance—The JOY-Filled Life* (Minneapolis: Bethany House Publishers, 1984), p. 23.

8. Ibid., p. 28.

9. Chuck Pierce is Vice President of Global Harvest Ministries (founded by Peter Wagner) in Colorado Springs, Colorado. He is President of Glory of Zion International Ministries, Denton, Texas, and is affiliated with the World Prayer Center in Colorado Springs, Colorado.

Chapter 5: Intimacy with God

1. James Strong, *Strong's Exhaustive Concordance of the Bible* (Peabody, Mass.: Hendrickson Publishers, n.d.), *inhabit* (H#3427).

2. Tommy Tenney, *God's Favorite House* (Shippensburg, Pa.: Destiny Image Publishers, Inc., 1999), p. 56.

Chapter 6: The Breaker Anointing

1. James Strong, *Strong's Exhaustive Concordance of the Bible* (Peabody, Mass.: Hendrickson Publishers, n.d.), *breaker* (H#6555).

2. Matthew Henry, *A Commentary on the Whole Bible,* vol. 4 (Old Tappan, N.J.: Fleming H. Revell, n.d.), p. 1312.

3. Ibid.

Chapter 7: Prepare for Power

1. James Strong, *Strong's Exhaustive Concordance of the Bible* (Peabody, Mass.: Hendrickson Publishers, n.d.), *kindly* (KJV, *comfortably*) (H#3820).

2. Ibid., *Achor* (H#5911).

3. Ibid., *shakes* (KJV, *shaketh*) (H#2342).

4. Ibid., *kadesh* (H#6946).

Chapter 8: It's Time for Transformation

1. Ed Silvoso, *That None Should Perish* (Ventura, Calif.: Regal Books, 1994), p. 154.

2. James Strong, *Strong's Exhaustive Concordance of the Bible* (Peabody, Mass.: Hendrickson Publishers, n.d.), *kabod* (H#3519).

3. Tommy Tenney, *God's Favorite House* (Shippensburg, Pa.: Destiny Image Publishers, Inc., 1999), p. 49.

4. Ibid.

5. Ibid., p. 52.

6. *Webster's Revised Unabridged Dictionary* (MICRA, INC: 1996, 1998). Information found on www.dictionary.com.

7. Fuchsia Pickett, *Worship Him* (Lake Mary, Fla.: Creation House, 2000), p. 177.

8. Ibid., p. 140.

9. *American Heritage Dictionary of the English Language,* 4th ed. (New York: Houghton Mifflin Co., 2000).

10. *Women of Destiny Bible* (Nashville: Thomas Nelson, Inc., 2000), p. 838.

Chapter 9: Sowing with a View

1. James Strong, *Strong's Exhaustive Concordance of the Bible* (Peabody, Mass.: Hendrickson Publishers, n.d.), *photizo* (G#5461).

Chapter 10: The Roar of the Lion

1. *The Holy Bible, New American Standard* (Nashville: Broadman and Holman Publishers, 1977), p. 642. See the center column of Isaiah 61:1.

Chapter 11: Harvest Glory

1. *The American Heritage Dictionary,* see www.dictionary.com.

BIBLIOGRAPHY

Curran, Sue. *I Saw Satan Fall Like Lightning.* Lake Mary, Fla.: Creation House Publishers, 1998.

Henry, Matthew. *A Commentary on the Whole Bible.* 6 vols. Old Tappan, N.J.: Fleming H. Revell, n.d.

Kilpatrick, John. *When the Heavens Are Brass.* Shippensburg, Pa.: Destiny Image Publishers, Inc., 1997.

Pickett, Fuchsia. *Worship Him.* Lake Mary, Fla.: Creation House Publishers, 2000.

Schlink, M. Basilea. *Repentance—The JOY-Filled Life.* Minneapolis: Bethany House Publishers, 1984.

Sheets, Dutch. *The River of God.* Ventura, Calif.: Renew Books, A Division of Gospel Light, 1998.

Silvoso, Ed. *That None Should Perish.* Ventura, Calif.: Regal Books, 1994.

Strong, James. *Strong's Exhaustive Concordance of the Bible.* Peabody, Mass.: Hendrickson Publishers, n.d.

Tenney, Tommy. *The God Catchers.* Nashville: Thomas Nelson Publishers, 2000.

———. *God's Favorite House.* Shippensburg, Pa.: Destiny Image Publishers, Inc., 1999.

Women of Destiny Bible. Nashville: Thomas Nelson, Inc., 2000.

LaNora Van Arsdall has been gifted by the Lord with a dynamic prophetic ministry. She travels and ministers nationally and internationally declaring God's Word with the revelation the Lord has given her. Her message has brought breakthroughs to the lives of both individuals and churches.

LaNora, who has degrees in communications and theology, pastored with her husband, Dan, for seventeen years and has previously served the Spiritual Warfare Network and Iverna Tompkins' ministry. In 2000 LaNora launched Fountaingate Ministries International with the dual vision of uniting ministries and pastors and transforming cities through presence evangelism.

LaNora and Dan reside in Mesa, Arizona. They have two daughters, Melanie and Kari. Melanie has two children, Meshea and Riley, and serves as the worship coordinator for Fountaingate. Kari and her husband, Tim, have one son, Noah, and pastor Fountain of Life Church in Gilbert, Arizona.

For more information or for bookings contact:

LaNora Van Arsdall
Fountaingate Ministries International
P.O. Box 1333
Gilbert, AZ 85299-1333
Phone: 1-877-658-8388